MARK DICK

TOWARDS
OIKOS

A revalued perspective on global inequality and global warming

For Colin, Peter, and Martin

There are ninety and nine who live and die
In want and hunger and cold
That one many live in luxury
And be wrapped in silken fold.
The ninety and nine in hovels bare
The one in a palace with riches rare …
And the one owns cities, houses and lands
And the ninety and nine have empty hands.

The Farmers' Alliance, 31 July 1889 at Populist Revolt, USA

Mark Dick *is a Northern Ireland General Medical Practitioner, graduated from Queen's University Belfast in 1986, lives in Ballymena, has interests in sport and volunteering via Scouting and is a member of First Presbyterian Church, Ballymena.*

Published 2019 by Dr CM Dick
©2019 All rights reserved
ISBN 978-1-5272-4825-0

Designed by April Sky Design, Newtownards
www.aprilsky.co.uk

Printed by GPS Colour Graphics Ltd, Belfast

CONTENTS

INTRODUCTION

'DOCTOR, THE WAITING LIST is over two years to have my hip replacement! Why should I have to go privately when I have paid my "stamp" all these years and I am in so much pain?' As a General Practitioner, I frequently hear this angry refrain these days. It always provokes a frustrated, unspoken response in my head: 'But the country is "bankrupt" – in the sense that the UK has a huge public debt – at least you will get a hip replacement; many, across the world, are not so fortunate'. Thinking more deeply, I realise it is actually quite difficult for patients or any individual to embrace global economic concepts that seem to have no direct relevance to themselves. In many instances we all think from inside our little bubble. Issues of inequality of opportunity, wealth and power, of environmental stewardship, of fair distribution of resources, of decision making in politics and of sustainability of lifestyles are all concepts which require consideration. Many never take the time to consider these issues, and those people who do often argue round and round in circles, debating aspects of economics and money, finally blaming everything on human nature. I want to consider and examine all the issues that lie behind the delivery of a seemingly straightforward elective surgery for an expensive joint operation. This involves breaking out of our individual bubbles to consider two of the biggest existential threats to humanity. Firstly, we must consider the social injustice inherent in the current disparities of wealth, income and power, which may well lead to conflict between economic groupings. Secondly, we must consider how to address climate change which if unchecked will spell disaster for all of us in the future.

Meanwhile, humanity is making progress, or so it is claimed, in terms of absolute poverty, health, education, democracy and freedom in many parts of the world. However, it is time for the world, particularly the Western world, to consider these issues of social justice and ecological damage. Decisions made now, or not made now, will have profound consequences for future generations. There are many important conflating perspectives for consideration, including a new (revalued) standard of living for humankind, a 'restructured economy' worldwide challenging the Western status quo and a further 'greening' of the debate.

Over ten years since the financial crash of 2008, much discussion centres around which economies have managed to return to their pre-2008 position. Estimates are made as to how much economic growth has been lost over the past ten years. Surely there is a more important and far-reaching question to ask. Why has the huge disparity in wealth, income and power that characterised the end of the nineteenth century reoccurred again in the twenty-first century? This book is part of a search to answer that question and then to find out if there are any solutions to social injustice and ecological damage.

Mervyn King, former Governor of the Bank of England, writes well and knowledgeably in his 2016 book *The End of Alchemy* (on money, banking and the future of the global economy) but has little to say about the poverty in the Third World or man's interaction with nature. The Reverend Graham Beynon, Minister of Grace Church, Cambridge, UK, in his little booklet *Money Counts* (2016), has much advice to offer about money and life on a personal level – his thoughts are challenging for everyone, from those on high incomes to those not so well off and everyone in between. Neither book comments much on the effects of modern life on the ecology of the earth, but Kate Raworth, an English economist working at the University of Oxford, does so in *Doughnut Economics* (2017). Whether her optimism overcomes the pessimism of Paul Kingsnorth, former deputy editor of *The Ecologist*, in *Confessions of a Recovering Environmentalist* (2017) is open to debate. I want to link these ideas together and draw also on the thoughts of the agrarian environmentalist Wendell Berry (*The World-Ending Fire*, 2017) and the economist and politician Yanis Varoufakis (*And the Weak Suffer What They Must?*, 2016). It is also important to balance Paul Kingsnorth's pessimism with a glass-half-full person like Steven Pinker (Johnstone Family Professor, Department of Psychology, Harvard University). He really does believe in human progress using the legacy of the Enlightenment as his foundation. In *Enlightenment Now* (2018) he describes the Enlightenment era as a collection of ideas, some of them contradictory, from which four themes emerge: reason, science, humanism and progress. Rutger Bregman, the Dutch historian, in his 2018 book *Utopia for Realists*, feels people and politicians should look again at three radical ideas: (1) a universal basic income, (2) a shorter workweek and (3) open borders. To which I would add, in agreement with Professor Thomas Piketty, Paris School of Economics: (4) a progressive global tax on capital – the rationale for which he clearly outlined in *Capital in the Twenty-First Century* (2014).

All these books look at the world from a slightly different viewpoint. *The*

End of Alchemy majors on the build-up to and the resulting chaos from the 2008 financial crisis. *Confessions of a Recovering Environmentalist* is quite pessimistic about the 'green movement's' drift towards technological fixes for the looming climate change disaster. While acknowledging the looming disaster, *Doughnut Economics* at least sets out some possible solutions. Yanis Varoufakis focuses on a functioning or non-functioning European Union and his book is an account of how the forces of capital have prevailed over the common good. Wendell Berry, through a series of essays spanning over 40 years, has some very thought-provoking things to say about man's relationship with nature and he and Kingsnorth find much in common. Pinker makes great use of the Oxford economist Max Roser's *Our World in Data* to make the case for progress. As you would expect, Beynon diverges from humanism and points to where ultimately he feels real power, authority and control lies. Bregman asks why it is that so many good ideas don't get taken seriously? Well, politicians cannot adopt viewpoints that are too extreme. Joseph Overton, an American lawyer, realised that there was a window of acceptability. The media gatekeepers will quickly brand anyone who operates outside this window as 'unrealistic' or 'unreasonable'. Television often offers little time or space to present fundamentally different opinions. The 'Overton Window' can shift though. There are probably more folk out there with interesting new ideas than people realise. It was such folk, with thick skins, who called for the abolition of slavery and for universal suffrage after all. One person with a thick skin was Tony Atkinson. In his book *Inequality: What can be done?* Professor Atkinson (and also Thomas Piketty in *Capital in the Twenty-First Century* for that matter) takes a detailed look at inequality – its diagnosis and some proposals for action – mainly from a Western world viewpoint. The book that most matches my attempt to think globally is *The Divide* by Jason Hickel in 2017.

My book sets out, with the help of these and other authors, to examine many aspects of inequality (social injustice) and ecological damage (climate change), and then to look at how they interact. Chapter 1 reintroduces the model of Doughnut Economics for the modern world and the search for a safe and just space for all. Chapter 2 explains why we need to find some better metrics than the flawed Gross Domestic Product or Gross National Income. Chapter 3 looks in detail inside the inner ring of the Doughnut at the scandal of inequality. To go any way down the road of addressing inequality worldwide, the concept of limits across many dimensions is presented in Chapter 4. Then Chapter 5 discusses whether economics at different levels is a simple subject or rather complex. The unavoidable topics of redistribution and regeneration are tackled in Chapter 6; and as these are deeply unsettling for many, Chapter 7 outlines the huge problems there will be in instituting good governance and decision making across global communities in the future. Many of these decisions involve the ecology of the planet and Chapters 8 and 9 challenge the gospel of economic growth and burst some 'bubbles' that bedevil many peoples' self-centred outlook. Chapter 10 goes in search of some real solutions to the issues raised by inequality and ecological damage. The best ideas are presented in the appendix 1 spreadsheet. They all point to a revalued standard of living.

I have been heavily influenced by Kate Raworth's thinking but have not intended to undertake a grand exercise in plagiarism; rather a blending together of the best thoughts and ideas from many sources, in search of some wisdom, in relation to inequality (social injustice) and ecological damage (climate change). *Oikos* is the ancient Greek word for family, family property and the household home. This book is about a scaled up version of these concepts (economy and ecology): namely the whole human family as equals, the distribution of wealth and our planetary home. Knowledge and wisdom are not the same. There is wisdom contained in The Lord's Prayer. From a Christian viewpoint, the essence of this book is about The Kingdom of God, which does not have to be delayed until some time in the distant future. The Kingdom of God should also be about here and now:

Our Father which art in heaven,
Hallowed be Thy name.
Thy Kingdom come, Thy will be done on earth, as it is in heaven.
Give us this day our daily bread,
And forgive us our debts, as we forgive our debtors.
And lead us not into temptation, but deliver us from the evil:
For Thine is the Kingdom, and the power, and the glory, forever.
Amen.
(Matthew 6:9–13 and Luke 11:1–4; *The Bible*)

I have combined part of the prayer with the meaning behind *oikos* to obtain a title for this search for a different, revalued standard of living. In conclusion, I give a personal reflection on the two great commandments of honouring God in His creation (ecology) and honouring our neighbours (economy).

CHAPTER 1

GLOBALISATION AND DOUGHNUT ECONOMICS

FIRST, LET US CONSIDER how we might address these two existential threats (inequality and climate change) without playing one off against the other. King feels, 'Over many years, a capitalist economy has proved the most successful route to escape poverty and achieve prosperity'. Not all across the world have benefited. But certainly 'the West has successfully built the institutions to support a capitalist system – the rule of law, property rights, intellectual freedom, anti-monopoly regulation, and collective infrastructure (education, water, electricity and telecommunications)' (King, 2016). Pinker agrees (the full title of his book is *Enlightenment Now: The Case for Reason, Science, Humanism and Progress*) that humanity has never had it so good. He uses global data to argue his manifesto that the good guys have already won and provides grounds for an optimistic future. Violence and the conditions that have promoted it have decreased. Many humans live longer and are better fed. Epidemic disease, famine, infant mortality and childbirth deaths have declined. Literacy and education are more widespread (Pinker, 2018). Our trust in reason, science and industry has brought dividends to some. However, in *The Divide*, Jason Hickel would contend that the scorebook for poverty depends on where the line is drawn – living on $1 per day or $5 per day. Since 1960, the income gap between the North and South has roughly tripled in size. Today, 4.3 billion people – sixty per cent of the world's population – live on less than $5 per day. Some 1 billion live on less than $1 a day (Hickel, 2017).

Berry also has a much more critical view of this industrialisation. He has a deep love of soil and place. Industrialism prescribes an economy that is placeless and displacing. It often does not distinguish one place from another. It thus continues the economy of colonialism. Colonialism made some distinctions very sharply: the mining and extractive economies of South Africa and Zambia, versus the white farmers of Kenya, show very different forms of economic management. The shift of colonial power from European monarchy to global corporations is perhaps the dominant theme of modern history. The colonisation of the entire rural world by global corporations has been the same story of gathering an exploitive economic power into the hands of a few people who are alien to the place and the people they exploit. Such an economy is bound to destroy locally adapted agrarian economies everywhere it goes, simply because it is too ignorant not to do so (Berry, 2017).

The economic doughnut

From a Christian perspective, Beynon would also challenge our modern attitudes, particularly towards money, progress and altruism – how do we decide what to spend and what to spend it on, how do we decide what to give and where to give it, and how do we decide what to save and what to save it for? Rarely does anyone come to a pastor saying that they have a problem with handling money ('please help me with my greed'). But what we should want is no one in great poverty or distress when others have more than they need. There is surely a great challenge for those of us who live in the prosperous West ('the Land of Plenty' is Bregman's phrase) to relieve the needs of fellow human beings elsewhere in the world (Beynon, 2011). The world is about one hundred times wealthier than it was two centuries ago. But in his 1977 book, *Rich Christians in an Age of Hunger*, Ron Sider, the Canadian-American theologian, talks about a billion hungry neighbours. He divides the world up, as other have done, into low-income countries (847 million) like Bangladesh and Malawi; lower middle-income countries (2.5 billion) like Bolivia and Vietnam; upper middle-income countries (2.4 billion) like Brazil and China; and high-income countries (1.3 billion) like Norway and USA (Sider, 2015). This theme is picked up by Raworth in the first part of *Doughnut Economics*. Many millions of people still lead lives of extreme deprivation. Worldwide, one person in nine does not have enough to eat. The world is still extraordinarily unequal: as of 2015 the world's richest ten per cent now own more wealth than the other ninety per cent put together (Raworth, 2017).

The theme for the second part of *Doughnut Economics* is that human activity is putting unprecedented stress on Earth's life giving systems. Paul Kingsnorth would certainly agree. His pessimism can be overwhelming; the complete opposite of Steven Pinker. *'If you don't despair, in times like these, you are not fully alive. But there has to be something beyond despair too; or rather, something that accompanies it, like a companion on the road – the development of a philosophy for a dark time; a dark ecology. None of it is going to save the world – but then there is no saving the world, and the ones who say there is are the ones you need to save it from!'* (Kingsnorth, 2017).

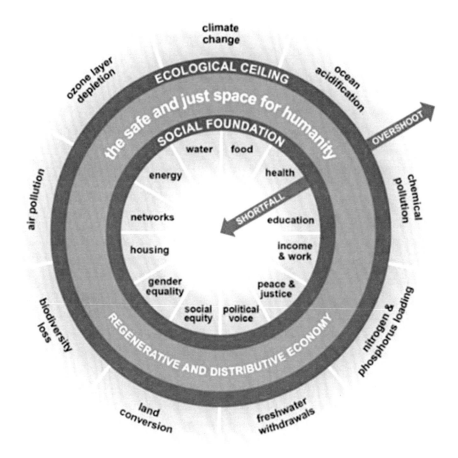

Kate Raworth is not defeated and rolls her sleeves up with some ideas …

The essence of her Doughnut model is a social <u>foundation</u> of well-being that no one should fall below, and an ecological <u>ceiling</u> of planetary pressure that we should not go beyond. Between the two lies a safe and just space for all (Raworth, 2017). It is basically a call for a race to the middle and a <u>revalued standard of living for all.</u>

Matt Williams, a PhD student at St John's College, Durham, is recently returned from missionary work in Malawi. He writes in the Presbyterian Herald magazine:

> 'Poverty dominates life in Malawi. A self-giving response to Christ's love is required. 'If anybody has the world's goods and sees his brother in need, yet closes his heart against him, how

does the love of God dwell in him?' (1 John 3:17). The message is fairly simple; the gospel cannot be 'spiritualised' so as to exclude practical action. Some say that being poor is no problem and it can even make people more spiritual, but such people should start by considering the energy they expend ensuring that they are not poor. Besides, we are not talking about 'simple' or 'humble' living; a high proportion of the population in Malawi lives without adequate food and clothing. The Bible teaches contentment with minimum needs, not chronic malnutrition (1 Timothy 6:6–8) (Williams, 2016).'

This issue should be climbing to the top of everyone's agenda. But that could also have been said forty or fifty years ago! Unfortunately it is not a priority for an awful lot of people. However, population movements and competition for resources will not go away. Globalisation and the control of money and land are central issues.

Nobel Prize-winning economist Joseph Stiglitz outlined the problems our rapidly integrating world was facing in *Globalization and Its Discontents* in 2002. Many of the analyses and criticisms that he made have been accepted by world leaders. Then, in *Making Globalization Work* (2006), he proposes solutions and looks to the future. He notes the Washington Consensus (US Treasury, IMF, World Bank) prescription is based on a theory of the market economy that assumes perfect information, perfect competition, and perfect risk markets – an ideal of reality, which is of little relevance to developing countries in particular.

In 1944, after the Bretton Woods Conference, the International Monetary Fund (IMF) was set up and charged with stability of the global financial system and the World Bank was charged with promoting development. The United States rejected the proposal for an International Trade Organisation in 1950 because of concerns on the part of some conservatives and corporations that it would lead to an infringement of national sovereignty and excessive regulation. It was not until 1995 that the World Trade Organisation (WTO) came into being. Stiglitz provided a devastating critique of these organisations (Stiglitz, 2002).

Trade agreements have made policies for promoting technology, closing the knowledge gap, and using financial markets as catalysts for growth more difficult, if not impossible, for developing countries to pursue. In part, free trade has not worked because it has not been tried: trade agreements of the past have been neither free nor fair. They have been asymmetric, opening up markets in the developing countries to goods from advanced countries without full reciprocation (Stiglitz, 2006).

Berry exposes the contrast between global industrialisation and the small family farm. In so many areas, industrialisation has moved employment and work away from the home, adding many unproductive journeys in the process. In many countries soil loss, genetic impoverishment and groundwater pollution have become large-scale problems, which will be difficult to reverse. Far too often globalisation consumes valuable resources without any thought for the future and gives nothing in return. Modern economies' most voluminous product is waste – valuable materials are irrecoverably misplaced, or randomly discharged as poisons (Berry, 2017). However, Berry can be somewhat backward looking, focusing on small, family-run, self-sufficient food-producing entities which are difficult to place sensibly in twenty-first century economics, where the vast majority of populations will live in cities.

As mentioned above, Bregman uses the phrase 'the Land of Plenty' to describe the affluent developed world. But he believes that there is a dearth of ideas to push humanity forwards to new utopias. '*Notching up our purchasing power another percentage point, or shaving a couple off our carbon emissions; perhaps a new gadget – we live in an era of wealth and overabundance for some. The real crisis is that we cannot come up with anything better*' (Bregman, 2018). There is an urgent need to share more evenly the bounty of planet Earth.

Naomi Klein, the Canadian journalist and writer, has identified this urgent need in her book, *This Changes Everything*. She believes the idea that capitalism and only capitalism can save the world from a climate crisis created by unrestrained capitalism is a theory that has been tested and found wanting. Celebratory billionaires, with their near mystical quests for energy 'miracles', tap into what may be our culture's most intoxicating narrative: the belief that technology is going to save us from the effects of our actions (Klein, 2014).

Meanwhile, globalisation and unrestrained capitalism march on regardless, driven by the banking systems of the world. Central bank independence, the free flow of capital and the removal of banking regulations led to three consequences, according to King. The Good was a period of stability from 1990 to 2007. The Bad was the rise in debt levels. The Ugly was the development of an extremely fragile banking system in 2007–8 (King, 2016). All of this played out on a national or international level, but on a more individual level, Beynon intuitively knows that money also has an enduring importance: '*Some of us would like to escape money and banks altogether. It is a source of annoying decisions, boring lists, family arguments and maybe paralysing anxiety. Money keeps some awake at night. For others it is a source of new opportunities, exciting prospects, the promise of comfort and maybe reassuring security. Money helps some sleep at night'* (Beynon, 2011). But for large swathes of the world's population, who have very little money, life is a hand-to-mouth existence with no safety net.

Social justice demands that both ends of Beynon's spectrum are addressed. Every human being is surely entitled to a fair share of the world's God-given resources. This should not simply be dictated by whether you are born in the USA or Bangladesh. A transfer of wealth across the world in the name of fairness means a **revalued standard of living/lifestyle for all** that does not contravene planetary boundaries. So next we need to think about how we measure our standard of living.

CHAPTER 2

GROSS DOMESTIC PRODUCT

THE CURRENT METRICS THAT we use to assess progress need a rethink. Raworth's **first** new thought would be to **change from the goal of growth (GDP) to the Doughnut model.** The four major components of Gross Domestic Product are personal consumptive expenditures, investment, net exports and government expenditure. Increasing Gross Domestic Product (GDP) is virtually worshipped by Western politicians. It allows them to dream of a future where they will be able to indulge a wish list, promising an improved standard of living for their populations. To argue against this is currently political suicide. Little thought is given to working out if populations can thrive without necessarily growing. But this is the essence of the Doughnut model (moving to a safe and just space) – pointing towards a different future where every person's needs are provided for, while still safeguarding the living world on which we all depend. Surely it is an admirable goal to attempt to lift all human beings out of absolute poverty while also avoiding more ecological damage (Raworth, 2017). These are not new ideas. Robert Kennedy's speech at Kansas University in 1968 pointed out the idiocy of GDP as a metric: 'GDP measures neither our wit nor our courage, neither our wisdom nor our learning, neither our compassion nor our devotion to our country, it measures everything in short, except that which makes life worthwhile.' (Kennedy, 2012).

And King Wangchuck of Bhutan argued in 1972 for a Gross National Happiness Index – he was mocked mercilessly but his ideas are now being revisited.

Wendell Berry would expand this and say ... *'our current fearful predicament calls for much prudence, humility, good work and propriety of scale. It calls for a revalued standard of living. It calls for the complex responsibilities of caretaking and the giving-back that we mean by 'stewardship'. The issue of limitation is critical – 'this much and no more' (… only so much land, so much water, so much hay in the barn, so much firewood in the shed, so much food in the cellar, so much strength in the arms, etc.). This is exactly opposite to global industrialism. Striving for more and more 'growth' violates all limits. Whether by promoting personal mobility, extractive machinery, long-distance transport and scientific/technological breakthroughs, the quest for GDP growth stretches the ecology of the planet beyond breaking point. In the absence of this 'growth', this greed and this affluence, the landless dependents of an industrial economy too easily suffer the consequences of having no land: joblessness, homelessness and want'.* (Berry, 2017).

In this regard, it is relevant that Paul Kingsnorth reminds us about the progress trap. (Kingsnorth, 2017). In his book *A Short History of Progress*, Ronald Wright coined the term 'progress trap'. A progress trap is a short-term social or technological improvement that turns out in the longer term to be a backward step. By the time this is realised – if it ever is – it is too late to change course. Each improvement tends to make society bigger, more complex, less human-scale, more destructive to non-human life and more likely to collapse under its own weight (Wright, 2004).

Steven Pinker is much more positive and rages against what he describes as 'progressophobia'. It is the idea of progress that rankles with the chattering classes – the Enlightenment belief that by understanding the world we can improve the human condition. Intellectuals and ordinary people both can experience improvements in their individual lives, yet when considering society as a whole they transform from Tigger to Eeyore (The Optimism Gap). 'Bad is stronger than good.' News outlets have become gloomier and gloomier from the late 1970s to the present day. But pessimism has a bright side! The expanding circle of sympathy makes some of us concerned about harms that would have passed unnoticed in more callous times.

A simple version of Maslow's hierarchy of needs has five levels – physiological needs, safety needs, belongingness needs, esteem needs and, at the top, self-actualisation needs. Most people prioritise life, health, safety, literacy, sustenance, and stimulation (the lower levels of Maslow's pyramid) before transcendent religious or romantic values like salvation, grace, sacredness, heroism, honour, glory and authenticity. And the world, in the form of UN Millennium Development Goals, agrees. The shock is that the world has generally made progress in measures of human well-being but almost no one knows about it (Pinker, 2018). Obviously there have been bumps along the road.

The Land of Plenty

It is a privilege of the rich to rank other goals ahead of growth. But for most of the world's population, money takes the cake. 'There is only one class in the community that thinks more about money than the rich', said Oscar Wilde, 'and that is the poor'. In the Land of Plenty, we need different metrics. Modern journalism would be all but lost without GDP, wielding the latest national growth figures as a kind of government report card. It is hard to believe that eighty years ago GDP did not even exist. The meaning of the term 'national income' has actually never been fixed, fluctuating with the latest intellectual currents. Eventually, in trying to answer the simple question, 'How much stuff can we make?' Simon Kuznets, a young Russian professor, laid the foundations of what would later become GDP. It is the ultimate yardstick in times of war but not so much in peacetime.

> '*When the United Nations published its first standard guideline for figuring GDP in 1953, it totalled just fewer than fifty pages. The most recent edition, issued in 2008, comes in at 722 pages... To calculate the GDP, numerous data points have to be linked together and hundreds of wholly subjective choices made and yet it is always presented as hard science, which can influence political re-election or annihilation'.(Bregman, 2018).*
>
> *Every era needs its own figures. In the eighteenth century, they concerned the size of the harvest. In the nineteenth century, the extent of the rail network, the number of factories and the volume of coal mining. And in the twentieth century, industrial mass production within the boundaries of the nation state. But today in a service-based economy, simple quantitative targets fail. The Genuine Progress Indicator (GPI) has actually receded in the USA since the 1970s. The Index of Sustainable Economic Welfare (ISEW) incorporates pollution, crime, inequality and volunteer work in its equations. The Happy Planet Index is a ranking that factors in ecological footprints, in which most developed countries figure somewhere around the middle and the USA dangles near the bottom. In fact, simple rankings consistently conceal more than they reveal. We are living in an information age where we spend increasing amounts of money on activities about which we have little solid information (Bregman, 2018).*

In Bhutan, 'Gross National Happiness' is still more important than 'Gross Domestic Product'. The concept implies that sustainable development should take a holistic approach towards notions of progress and give equal importance to non-economic aspects of well-being. The idea of Gross National Happiness (GNH) has influenced Bhutan's economic and social policy, and also captured the imagination of others far beyond its borders. In creating the Gross National Happiness Index, Bhutan sought to create a measurement tool that would be useful for policymaking and create policy incentives for the government, NGOs and businesses of Bhutan to increase GNH.

The GNH Index includes both traditional areas of socio-economic concern, such as living standards, health and education, and less traditional aspects of culture and psychological well-being. It is a holistic reflection of the general well-being of the Bhutanese population rather than a subjective psychological ranking of 'happiness' alone.

The GNH Index includes nine domains:
Psychological well-being
Health
Education
Time use
Cultural diversity and resilience
Good governance
Community vitality
Ecological diversity and resilience
Living standards

The most recent examples of progress followed by collapse would be 1929 and 2007–08. Yet even King acknowledges that, since 2008, the developed world is still searching for a sustainable recovery (growth) despite cuts in interest rates and the printing of electronic money by central banks on an unprecedented scale. There are internal imbalances, with domestic spending too high (and saving too low) relative to current and prospective incomes. And there are external imbalances with large surpluses and deficits between different countries (King, 2016). Balance is important both on the macro-scale (international) and the micro-scale (personal). Yanis Varoufakis, Professor of Economics at the University of Athens and previously Finance Minister of Greece, feels Europeans have taken far too long to understand that 2008 is just a version of 1929. In 1929 protectionism took the form of devaluing one's currency vis-à-vis others. In 2010 it took the form of devaluing one's labour vis-à-vis others. It was not long before underpaid German workers hated the Greeks and underemployed Greek workers hated the Germans. 'A debt is a debt is a debt!' was what a high-ranking official of the Federal Republic of Germany told him during his first official visit to Berlin. Just as in Germany, once the euro crisis erupted and it was considered self-evident that the Greeks were insufferable debtors, so too in Greece, Germany's unpaid wartime debts may remain forever unforgiven. The last thing he needed was this clash of moralising narratives. A debt may be a debt, but an unpayable debt does not get paid unless it is sensibly restructured. Neither German teenagers in 1953 – when the United States 'wrote down' Germany's public debt to, among other nations, Greece – nor Greek teenagers in 2010 deserved a life of misery because of unpayable debts amassed by a previous generation (Varoufakis, 2016). More globally there are ongoing arguments for reparations, for example, Nigeria's call for a practical recompense from the developed world over the depredations of slavery.

Varoufakis feels capitalism flourished only after debt was 'de-moralised'. He feels that restructuring Greece's public debt is essential for creating the growth spurt necessary to help repay her debts (Varoufakis, 2016). 'Onwards and upwards' has taken us into dangerous terrain though. GDP growth is no longer a good enough proxy for progress. Now good progress should be defined as 'coming into dynamic balance'. What if we each were to mentally map our own lives onto the Doughnut, asking ourselves: how does the way I shop, eat, travel, earn a living, bank, vote and volunteer affect my personal impact on the social and planetary boundaries (Raworth, 2017)? It is too easy to live in a self-centred bubble. We think it is our money. We earned it, we own it, we can do as we please with it. But perhaps Christians are on the right track, breaking out of the bubble, by believing everything belongs to God (Beynon, 2011) and believing every lifestyle action affects everyone else to some degree.

Rebuilding after a disaster provides a terrific impetus for an economy. So should we welcome climate disasters (e.g. Japanese tsunami of 2011) or world wars? Of course not – the *nature* of economic activity is vital and of course modern society's sacred measure of progress, the GDP, does not include community service, clean air, free refills on the house, and housework itself! The Greek GDP spiked twenty-five per cent when its black market economy was included. The GDP also does a poor job of calculating advances in knowledge. Stunning technological advances figure as little more than pocket change in the GDP. Mental illness, obesity, pollution, crime – in terms of GDP, it is the more the better. The GDP is indifferent to inequality, and to debts, which makes living on credit a tempting option (Bregman, 2018).

Berry notes that apologists of globalisation say that industrialisation of agriculture and its dominance by corporations has been 'inevitable'. They also say that industrial agriculture has come about by 'choice', inspired by compassion to 'feed the world'. We need to notice that these two arguments exactly contradict each other. The question is not how the world will be fed, but who will control the land and therefore the wealth of the world. If one sees the advantages of local economies and eliminating waste, and the cruelties of landlessness and homelessness, then one might reasonably hope to solve problems by achieving harmony and balance. For a few powerful people to own or control all land and worship a growing GDP is tragic (Berry, 2017). However, Berry needs to remember that not every local situation has optimal factors for agricultural production, especially if your nation state is all Sahara desert, Gobi tundra or Arctic wastes.

Health care in the Land of Plenty
Governments need to remember harmony and balance also. A government spending money that in reality it does not have is wrong. In the UK, for instance, government spending on the National Health Service is out of control, sucking in more and more resources. Sensible balance has been lost. A whole-scale root and branch rethink is required in many areas of modern life and health care is just one aspect. In the United Kingdom, changing to a private model for general practice care, for example, is unlikely to be effective without changes to other parts of the NHS. If you tinker with just one aspect of the system, there is likely to be a period of chaos as patients try to access free care elsewhere at Out Of Hours (OOH) and A&E (**A**nything **&** **E**verything!) These services could collapse with the government left blaming doctors. But neither can the status quo continue for much longer. Radical change in primary care provision has to come from central government as planned policy, and not just from hundreds of individual GP practices muddling through.

Douglas Higgs, the Director of the MRC Molecular Haematology Unit at the University of Oxford, agrees that there needs to be more honesty surrounding the NHS. He feels:

> *...Recent 'experts' have been depressingly superficial and made the same economic error as those setting up the NHS: namely that improving the health and longevity of the population would ultimately reduce cost. The opposite is true. If people die prematurely, they cost the NHS nothing. The NHS is a victim of its own fantastic success, but the cost is rising exponentially. Prevention and looking after one's own health is a priority, but the reality is that we all get sick – costing the NHS – and then die, no matter how well we look after ourselves. The idea that personalised*

medicine will decrease the bill is ludicrous. For example, patients shown (using genetic analysis) to have particular subtypes of tumours, will be eligible for treatments that cost tens of thousands of pounds per course, extending lives by up to a few years, with attendant healthcare problems. Equally, the idea of creating better links between hospitals and social services is all well and good, but where do family responsibilities come into this? We need an honest debate about what the NHS can and cannot deliver within a reasonable budget and how it should be rationed (Higgs, 2018).

In his book, *Homo Deus* (2015) Yuval Harari suggests that the rich will capture the benefits of high-tech, personalised medicine whilst the poor will have to make do with basic support.

A middle-way solution is needed. The NHS concept of 'free at the point of delivery' is overdue for review. The rising demand for primary care services needs to be curtailed (the 'tap needs turned off') by charging patients for ALL National Health Service activity at a rate of perhaps two per cent of actual costs – to include GP appointments, A&E, OOH, laboratory and radiology services, paramedical services, and prescriptions. This could be achieved without damaging health. Everything has intrinsic value. After these changes are introduced, General Medical Services remuneration could be reduced, also by two per cent. The government could adjust this 'point of service' charge up to 2.5% or down to 1.5% as necessary to balance the books.

There are other important issues at play here – growing antibiotic resistance being one. Some estimate that one in four antibiotic prescriptions issued by UK GPs are in fact unnecessary. Lack of understanding of the pathophysiology of viral infections and the fact that prescriptions are either free or attract only a nominal charge lead to a pressure to prescribe inappropriately. It is well known that GPs in busy practices, under constant time pressures, prescribe antibiotics more frequently than GPs with more time to properly educate patients. Some think that growing antibiotic resistance, if unchecked, will lead to the end of modern surgery. The NHS cannot continue on this path if disaster is to be avoided – change is urgently needed.

The social factors that influence health need to be given greater prominence. Sir Michael Marmot, Professor of Epidemiology and Public Health at University College London, has highlighted six such factors: early childhood years (SureStart), good education, sensible employment and working conditions, a universal basic income (considered in more detail later to advance equality of opportunity), healthy living spaces and political voice.

'It is only logical that we will continue to spend less on products that can be easily made more efficiently and spend more on labour-intensive services such as healthcare, education, safety and art. It is no accident that countries that score high on well-being, like Denmark, Sweden and Finland, have a large public sector. This is a blessing – the more efficient our technology, the more resources are left to attend to the old and infirm and to organise education on a more personal scale. The richer a country becomes the more it should be spending on teachers and doctors (Bregman, 2018).'

But there are limits. We will address this in Chapter 4. Whereas public sector services often bring a plethora of hidden benefits, the private sector is riddled with hidden costs. Governing by numbers is the last resort of a country that no longer knows what it wants, a country with no vision (Bregman, 2018).

'Have-not' health care

These factors apply all over the world. Dr Peter Rookes, University of Birmingham, has looked in some detail at the contribution of Christian Health Services in the developing world. In *Commitment, Conscience or Compromise: the changing financial basis and evolving role of Christian health services in developing countries,* he notes that health expenditure per capita ranges from (USD) $29 in Tanzania, $58 in Malawi, $91 in India, $147 in Papua New Guinea, $748 in South Africa, $2,560 in UK, to $3,294 in Iceland (Rookes, 2010).

The governments in both Malawi and India have produced strategic plans to deal with the deficiencies in their respective health sector delivery through managerial decentralisation, developing Primary Health Care, improving service access by poorer members of the community, cooperating with Non-State Providers (especially in Malawi: Christian Health Services) and improving regulation. The intention of the Sector-Wide Approach programmes in both countries is to involve key stakeholders in decisions about the allocation of resources. Christian Health Services (CHSs) are perceived as being stable and enduring, having generally originated from the mission hospitals founded in the nineteenth and twentieth centuries.

Major factors influencing whether governments engage with Christian Health Services appear to be, firstly the extent of CHSs' service contribution; second, whether CHSs are providing services not otherwise provided or in areas underserved by other providers; and third, the extent to which CHSs of different denominations cooperate (sometimes through a Christian Health Association – either a Coordinating CHA or Supporting CHA).

An increasing amount of health sector planning is devolved from national to regional governments in both Malawi and India. Despite CHSs providing up to fifty per cent of national health services in some countries, there is a major difference in the amount of material support various governments give to CHSs, ranging from virtually nothing up to full support including the payment of salaries and operational running costs, depending on the government's own economic position. Service agreements have been developed; for example, to reduce the high maternal and infant mortality rates in Malawi, District Health Officers (in areas where there are no accessible Government Health Service facilities) are negotiating service agreements with Christian Health Services to provide free antenatal care.

All of the health facilities researched in India and Malawi carry out some form of semi-coordinated community outreach in an attempt to avoid either neglect or duplication. But still many communities receive inadequate services.

There is concern, particularly in Malawi, that the decline in financial support from their partner mission organisations, exacerbated by the reduction in expatriate missionaries, could have a serious effect on the future viability of Christian Health Services and in turn increase pressure on Government Health Services. Unless funds from overseas are specifically designated for health, national churches do not seem to allocate them to CHSs.

Both in India and Malawi, as in a number of other countries, Government Health Services are technically free, although some facilities charge for particular components of treatment and some countries operate differential payment systems to encourage use of lower-level facilities. On the other hand, Christian Health Services in most countries must charge user fees to remain viable (in India 98–99%; in Malawi 20–50% of CHSs income). Many people either do not seek treatment, use self-medication, or attend traditional healers because they cannot afford CHS fees or the fare to travel to a Government Health Service (GHS) facility. There are strong views, even resentment, among community members and some government officials, that Malawian GHSs are perceived now to serve the poor and CHSs the middle class. In India, the quality of treatment provided by the for-profit institutions is, with notable exceptions, regarded as better than that provided by CHSs, but usually at a substantially higher cost. In Malawi, the quality of services provided by CHSs, including the attitudes of their staff, are generally regarded as superior to that of GHSs and the private for-profit sector. In the past, when CHSs were not controlled directly by governments there was a de-legitimisation of government service provision, with poor citizens comparing unfavourably their own government's performance with the relatively well-funded work of the CHSs and their international backers.

Churches and other faith-based organisations have played an important advocacy role. It is slowly being accepted that sustainable poverty reduction is only achievable by a more equitable approach to international trade and debt. However, there is also a need for strengthened political commitment to pro-poor economic growth, redistribution of resources and social protection policies within many of the countries concerned (Rookes, 2010).

Obviously all these important decisions need to be taken at a level above the regional departments of health, but rather by central governments. These are political decisions and need to be taken as part of an overall government strategy. But it should help motivate many to look after their own health rather than relying on the 'disease service' fixing them. In the UK, the present health service path is bankrupting the government coffers and will bankrupt other countries regardless of their GDP. Thriving balance is required personally, nationally and internationally. People need to consider a revalued standard of living/lifestyle for all.

Unrestrained capitalism and democracy

Kate Raworth asks: 'Can we live within the Doughnut worldwide?'

Moving into a safe and just space is determined by five factors: population, distribution, aspiration, technology and governance. The most effective way to stabilise the size of the human population is to ensure that every person can lead a life free of deprivation. Extremes of inequality push humanity beyond both sides of the Doughnut's boundaries. Commenting on city living, Tim Jackson (Professor of Sustainable Development at the University of Surrey) deftly states that we are 'persuaded to spend money we don't have on things we don't need to make impressions that won't last on people we don't care about' (Jackson, 2017). Jackson feels unrestrained capitalism is the main offender here, creating false wants and perpetuating 'false consciousness' when people view their own situations – they look up at those who have more and feel envious, but do not look down at those who have less and feel grateful. Urbanisation may fuel this consumerism but it also offers some technological opportunities to meet people's needs in far more effective ways. Designing governance that is suited to the challenges we face raises deep political issues that confront the long-standing interests and expectations of countries, corporations and communities alike (Raworth, 2017).

Pinker would suggest that it is easy to think that wealth has always been with us. History is written by the affluent with the leisure and education to do so. We celebrate those who lived well and forget those who lived in the silence of miserable poverty. Mythical golden ages of pastoral simplicity never existed.

> *'Among the brainchildren of the Enlightenment is the realisation that wealth is created and is not a fixed amount that has existed since the beginning of time. The Gross World Product today has grown almost a hundred fold since the Industrial Revolution. The quality of goods improves over time and technology invents new ones. How much did a laptop cost in 1800? The answer is no amount of money in the world. It is almost impossible to track material well-being across the decades and centuries. The paradox of value is that when an important good becomes plentiful, it costs far less than what people are willing to pay for it (economists often capture the price of everything and the value of nothing) (Pinker, 2018).'*

Some of the claims made by the United Nations Millennium Development Goals are strong and deserve to be celebrated. But the real story about global poverty is not quite as rosy. The World Bank changed several times the international poverty line and rebased the methodology for its calculation. Likewise, the definition of hunger did not take into consideration the difference in daily calories required for sedentary lifestyles as opposed to those needed for the arduous manual labour that most in the Global South endure. After forty years of anti-poverty efforts in sub-Saharan Africa, the World Bank projects that poverty numbers will have been 'reduced' from 287 million to 335 million people by 2030 (Hickel, 2017)!

The wealth that might have provided the capital for development in the Global South (precious metals and surplus labour) was effectively stolen by Europe and harnessed to the service of Europe's own development. Budding capitalists cannot get very far without sources of labour to work for wages. But peasant farmers cultivating the land to provide for their own needs do not want to work for wages, if they have secure access to land. The enclosure movement changed all this. Sheep and wool were the drivers in Britain. The application of market logic to land and farming marked the formal birth of capitalism. The Industrial Revolution then sucked desperate people into cities for work. The enormous wealth they produced was appropriated by the factory owners and created a 'trickle-up' effect!

Hickel feels there were internal and external conditions for the Industrial Revolution. It was three forces – enclosure, mass displacement of peasants and the creation of a consumer market – that created the internal conditions for the Industrial Revolution. The external conditions had to do with the colonisation of the Americas and the slave trade.

The process of enclosure (loss of access to land/commons) illustrates the basic logic of the process that would produce poverty across the rest of the world. Eventually Europe and the United States could siphon cheap raw materials from the periphery and then sell manufactured products back to the periphery while protecting themselves from competition by erecting high tariffs (Hickel, 2017). So far democracy has been weak at rebalancing these trends.

We will consider issues around democracy in some detail in Chapter 7. But in his book *Democracy and Its Crisis*, A C Grayling (Supernumerary Fellow at St Anne's College, Oxford) explains how the idea of representative democracy (defined later) emerged from a long debate (via Plato, Putney, Locke, Hobbes, Spinoza, Rousseau, Montesquieu, Madison, Constant, De Tocqueville, to John Stuart Mill's *Representative Government* in 1861) about how to make democracy work. Then Grayling discusses what has gone wrong with democracy, in the US and the UK (in his opinion, the Trump election and the Brexit decision being examples), and how he advises to put it right. Along the way he acknowledges Winston Churchill's less well-known quote that 'the strongest argument against democracy is a few minutes conversation with any voter' and H L Mencken's even more troubling observation that 'democracy is a pathetic belief in the collective wisdom of individual ignorance'. There are of course other types of governance that have been tried. The range can be summarised:

Aristocracy – rule by the best
Epistocracy – rule by knowledgeable experts
Timocracy – rule by those with property
Oligarchy – rule by the few (cabal/junta)
Plutocracy – rule by the rich over the poor
Democracy – rule by the whole populace (anarchy)
Ochlocracy – mob rule (Grayling, 2017)

Democracy is a relatively recent type of governance. Indeed, anarchy is the purest form of democracy. Voting systems, money (dark and otherwise) and disinformation mean that democracy might be mainstream but it is not necessarily offering people more influence over their politics. But democracy is still generally viewed as the best option. Two centuries ago only a handful of the world's countries were democratic. Now, two thirds are and Steven Pinker cites this as real progress because as a result discrimination against minorities is steadily declining. But for any form of governance to successfully lead to a safe and just place for all, the 'all' must come out of their self-centred bubbles and realise that the earth's resources need to be shared more equally. This is what 'globalisation' should really mean! Democracies need to acknowledge that GDP is a busted metric. There are better alternatives such as a Gross National Happiness Index or Genuine Progress Index, which will be discussed again and in more detail later. But first we need to take a detailed look at inequality in all its forms.

CHAPTER 3

INEQUALITY

IN 1973, P7 GEOGRAPHY textbooks talked about the 'haves' and the 'have-nots'. We, in the Western world (the 'haves'), are consuming more food, energy and other resources than would be sustainable if everybody in the whole world did the same. Are we engaging in trade relationships purely on the basis of what is good for us rather than what is fair for others (fairly traded, non-tariff, environmentally responsible goods)? It is not easy to vote to actively address chronic economic inequality as it is currently political suicide, in all countries, to stand up and say that there seems to be one rule for the international rich and another one for the extreme poor. While poor nations are forced to beggar themselves to service their unpayable debts, the world's biggest debtor, the United States, which owes trillions of dollars ($20 trillion, as of 2017), is left to its own devices: it suffers no externally imposed austerity programmes, inflation control or forced liberalisation.

> It is easy to assume that the divide between rich countries and poor countries has always existed. This notion sits at the centre of the usual story told about global inequality. If only poor countries would follow the advice of experts from agencies like the World Bank and the International Monetary Fund, they would gradually escape from poverty. But the story is wrong. In 1500, there was no appreciable difference in incomes and living standards between Europe and the rest of the world. Fortunes changed dramatically as Western powers exploited and coerced the rest of the world into a single international economic system (Hickel, 2017).
>
> Across the Global South during the 1950s, 1960s and 1970s, newly independent countries were ignoring the 'Washington consensus' advice and pursuing their own development agendas, building their economies with protectionist and redistributionist policies – trade tariffs, subsidies and social spending (actually following Western policies of the nineteenth century). Poverty rates were falling for the first time in history. But the profits of

Western corporations were being undermined, as was the access to cheap labour and resources. The era of the coup emerged in the 1980s when Western governments tried to bend everyone to their will.

Structural adjustment policies (SAPs) were sold as a necessary precondition for successful development but actually caused the opposite. By forcing open markets around the world, run by the World Trade Organisation, much damage was inflicted on poorer nations. Agricultural subsidies were abolished in the Global South but the US and the EU were allowed to continue subsidies to their own farmers. Poverty was recreated in the Third World. Today, $128 billion in international aid disbursements does exist, but this is vastly outstripped by the debt repayments, income from foreign investment and capital flight (trade mis-invoicing) flowing in the opposite direction (Hickel, 2017).

But we should all remember that the Internet and mobile phone technology is rapidly changing everything. In 1973 the 'haves' knew about the 'have-nots' but the 'have-nots' were not well informed about the 'haves'. Present migration trends from East to West and South to North suggest that the 'have-nots' are now realising that the 'haves' are keeping too much of 'The Kingdom's riches' to themselves. Thy Kingdom Come … should be for all! (Romans 15:27)

The tragedy of the commons
Raworth's **second idea** is to move from **the self-contained market of the twentieth century to an embedded economy in the twenty-first century**. She feels that during the twentieth century the neoliberal emphasis on the primacy of the free market has brought us to the brink of ecological, social and financial collapse. Historically the market has been given free rein because it is thought to be so efficient. But because it is so powerful it actually needs to be embedded in the economy wisely. Business has often been allowed to lead because it is innovative, but it needs to have well defined purpose. Trusting all finance institutions in an unlimited way is a mistake because they are not infallible; they should be made to serve society and not the other way round. Opening borders to make trade a 'win-win' can be a double-edged sword unless it is made fair. The state does not always have to be incompetent according to Raworth – she just wants to make it accountable. The household may have a domestic focus but it is still the core of human society the world

over, so its contribution should be valued in real terms. Society does exist and is foundational and all its connections should be nurtured. The commons (national, local and community institutions) are not all tragic failures, which have to be sold off; rather their creative potential should be unleashed. Power is pervasive so its abuse needs to be checked. And the twenty-first century needs to see the earth not as inexhaustible but as life-giving, and therefore its boundaries need to be respected (Raworth, 2017). The lack of egalitarian structures, so characteristic of neoliberal capitalism, and the forces behind economic exploitation must not be ignored. It is well recognised that in a shared-resource system, where individual users acting independently, according to their own self-interests, behave contrary to the common good of all users, and can end up depleting or spoiling that resource through their collective action. In 1968, ecologist Garrett Hardin explored this social dilemma his article '*The Tragedy of the Commons*', published in the journal *Science*. He promoted the adoption of policies which sensibility restrict private property and instead espouse expansion of public property for the common good (Hardin, 1968). Reflecting these constraints and enhancing a fair ethical capitalism based around a universal basic income (discussed in detail later) would help reduce inequality, and allow everyone to enter a safe and just space – an ethical race to the middle.

A clean atmosphere is a resource just like any other; there is a social cost to polluting, and people should have to pay the cost. After the Kyoto Protocol, there has to be a fair system of setting targets for all and there must be some way of enforcing them (trade sanctions, perhaps). Compliance will be much easier if the cost of reducing emissions is lowered, so we need to find ways of lowering these costs (Stiglitz, 2006).

John Carey's book review, in *The Sunday Times*, of Pinker's *Enlightenment Now* acknowledges that the Enlightenment perception that trade and commerce are less wasteful forms of international contact than warfare has at last filtered through to the world's leaders. So, fair and free trade should be part of the answer for the Third World also. There is much to be done in this regard. Historically both the UK and the US achieved global pre-eminence by ignoring fair trade rules, and now the major trading blocs – such as the EU, the US, etc. – do their utmost to push arrangements favourable to themselves rather than to notions of fairness more globally. There should be much value in work and earning money through work – given a level playing field in trade and commerce, unfortunately inequality is inbuilt into global society. Ha-Joon Chang's *23 Things They Don't Tell You About Capitalism* (2010) points out – in 'Thing 3' – that 'we have high salaries here for reasons of immigration control, not for reasons of hard work or skill or talent or diligence'. Although many in the West find it unpopular, open borders are actually the answer. We will return to this in Chapter 7.

The Western world has promoted the idea, post-World War II, of graciously relinquishing colonial power and turning to international aid to assist their fellow man. This story of development remains a compelling force in our society today with NGOs, philanthropic billionaires and media aid campaigns all involved in this enormous industry. Jason Hickel was able to analyse this development industry after joining World Vision. He discovered that their interventions were missing the point. The development industry wants the public to see that the gains in child and maternal mortality statistics are equivalent to overall success, but the public are not buying it because promises to End World Hunger and Make Poverty History remain unfulfilled (Hickel, 2017).

'Free trade'

Since the sixteenth century, mercantilism contended that military power came from wealth, and that wealth could be accumulated by minimising imports and maximising exports (admittedly at the point of a gun!) So colonial nations vied to control natural resources and captive markets for manufactured goods. This was certainly not 'free trade' – look at pirates and corsairs and the East India Company. The economist Adam Smith argued that nations got rich also by gains in productivity. In Britain, during 1848, the repeal of the Corn Laws ushered in the first so-called era of 'free trade'. Since then, trade has made some of the world much richer, as different nations gave up the attempt to be completely self-sufficient but instead began buying from others what they needed and specialising in what they did best. But 'free trade' also meant 'dispersed gains' and 'concentrated losses'. The first era of 'free trade' came to an end in 1929 when US farmers and industry demanded protection.

After 1947, first the General Agreement on Tariffs and Trade (GATT), followed by the World Trade Organisation (WTO), succeeded in bringing down tariffs but as an unfortunate side effect most developed nations have 'protected' themselves inside regional free-trade areas (EU, NAFRA, Mercosur). It should also be carefully noted that the WTO system allows national governments to suspend normal rules so as to protect their economies in certain circumstances (national security concerns, market disruption, unfair subsidised export practices and dumping goods below cost to drive out competition). Governments support free trade as long as it clearly benefits them. When threatened they tend to retreat into protectionism.

The World Trade Organisation draws its legitimacy from promising the right to engage in that most human of all activities – trading and bartering – without restriction. Yet in the past, strong protectionism and solid state support were the only paths to real industrial development.

The original General Agreement on Tariffs and Trade (GATT) began life rooted in Keynesian principles. But when the WTO was born in 1995, the neoliberal agenda dictated that it was designed to open up the world to capital flows from rich countries – an all-or-nothing deal. Under the Heckscher-Ohlin-Samuelson theory (developed on the ideas of British economist David Ricardo), each country should gravitate towards the things they are relatively better at, which should lead to increased efficiency. But the US Farm Bill and the EU Common Agricultural Policy do not sit well with the theory.

Cutting tariffs means losing customs tax revenue – one of the few easy sources of income for developing countries. Trade liberalisation directly denies poor countries the very resources they so desperately need to spend on social services and reducing poverty. Jobs and capital can just vanish overseas towards cheaper labour in a race to the bottom.

Within the WTO, G7 negotiators have a long history of convening special 'Green Room' meetings from which most developing countries and their advisers (if they can afford advisers) are excluded. Normally, states enjoy what is known as 'sovereign immunity' status, which means they cannot be sued. But this principle is suspended in cases of investor–state disputes, striking down the laws of sovereign states. States, on the other hand, cannot sue foreign investors, just nullify the lawsuit. Hearings are held in secrecy. This is an assault on democracy. Free-trade reforms have gradually dismantled sovereign 'capital controls'.

Money can be moved around the world at speed, posing severe threats to poor countries with a small capital base. International investors have immense power. Places with low wages, low taxes, cheap resources, and limited regulations on waste and pollution are favoured (Hickel, 2017).

The author George Monbiot, in his book *The Age of Consent*, addresses the issue of a Fair Trade Organisation as one of his three ideas for a manifesto for a new world order. He feels there are several preconditions for fair trade to allow the Third World to escape the poverty trap. Developing countries should be allowed limited temporary protectionism for their native industries. Strict conditions should be imposed on foreign investors so that they leave more wealth behind than they extract. The overriding of intellectual property rights should be the norm to allow catch-up. Hopefully, fewer foreign companies will need to be attracted by 'export processing zones' where unions are banned, pollution controls are scanty and few taxes are paid. Rich nations should operate open borders. Eventually, as development progresses, this positive discrimination can be reversed as the world progresses towards true free trade (Monbiot, 2003).

Matt Williams knows there is a long way to go:

> *We should at least have some grasp of why people are poor, and which practical avenues are open to us to respond, also remembering that there is something even more fundamental that can remain untouched, a root problem all but hidden beneath the surface of our hearts.*
>
> *So, what is this deep-seated problem? It is the sense of moral superiority. Before rushing to deny the charge, why not consider these questions:*
>
> - *Why do we really believe that poor people, especially in Africa, are poor whilst we are better off? 'Surely it is because they don't work as hard as us! We deserve what we have, but Africans seem to do little work and are neck-deep in corruption!'*
> - *What can we positively learn from Africa? Hmm… (The usual answer, reinforced in the national media, is 'Nothing').*
>
> *If we are honest, there is at least part of us that believes our country is in better condition because we are generally better people. But we should beware the temptation to assume that all the ugly parts of colonialism lie in the past as an unfortunate blip in our otherwise exemplary history. The fact is that one cornerstone of Western empires was a race-based sense of moral superiority and the remnants of this 'superiority' linger on (Williams, 2017).*

Edward Said, a Palestinian-American and Professor of Literature at Columbia University, outlines just this in *Orientalism* (1978) when he brilliantly examines how the West defined and thus created the non-West – the Orient and the status of alien peoples, including the ways we define ourselves as effortlessly superior. Said tries to help people look at things from the other's point of view to explain why injustices remain.

In a similar vein, Professor Kate Picket, Professor of Epidemiology, University of York, commented in the British Medical Journal recently:

Inequality is implicated in global risks, from fiscal crises to profound social instability, increasing polarisation of societies, increasing national sentiment, and even climate change and environmental degradation. This is because of the ways in which inequality drives consumerism and overconsumption. Economists have also identified the negative effect of inequality on economic stability and growth, as well as a negative effect on reducing poverty. You might think the evidence of harm would be enough to turn this problem around. But the long-term failure of governments to tackle these injustices is one of the reasons why public opinion has swung so strongly away from established politics. Now, more than ever, we need a vision of a future capable of creating more equal societies that increase sustainable wellbeing for all and for the planet (Picket, 2017).

Ginis, curves and waves

Inequality has traditionally been measured by the Gini coefficient (absolute range from 0–1). Developed by Italian statistician and sociologist Corrado Gini, it is a measure of relative inequality with values lying between 0 (complete equality, everyone gets the same income) and 1 (one person gets all the income). The Gini coefficient is defined as half the mean difference divided by the mean. Real-life range would be from 0.25 (egalitarian Sweden) to 0.7 (unequal South Africa). In the USA the share of income going to the richest one per cent grew from eight per cent in 1980 to eighteen per cent in 2015; what is morally important is that each should have enough. A damaging consequence of the lump fallacy is the belief that if some people get richer, they must have stolen more than their fair share from everyone else. But people are generally content with some economic inequality as long as they feel that the country is meritocratic, and they get angry when they feel it isn't. Politicians fell into the trap of using the word 'meritocratic' against the intentions of Michael Young, who wrote *The Rise of the Meritocracy* back in 1958 as a satire on non-meritocratic forms of advancement. Some degree of inequality is universal across societies, as is the awareness of inequality. Local awareness of some inequality has been the case historically also. In his book *Discourse on Inequality* in 1754, Rousseau set out to demonstrate how the growth of civilisation corrupts man's natural happiness and freedom by creating artificial inequalities of wealth, power and social privilege. Contending that primitive man was equal to his fellows, Rousseau believed that as societies become more sophisticated, the strongest and most intelligent members of the community gain an unnatural advantage over their weaker brethren, and that constitutions set up to rectify these imbalances through peace and justice in fact do nothing but perpetuate them. Rousseau's political and social arguments in the *Discourse* were a hugely influential denunciation of the social conditions of his time and the book was one of the most revolutionary documents of the eighteenth century.

Modern surveys of hunter-gatherer societies found that they were 'not quite in a state of "primitive communism"', but that the 'Ginis' averaged 0.33. James Suzman, an anthropologist specialising in the political economy of southern Africa, has examined the disappearing world of the Bushmen (especially the Ju|'hoansi of the Kalahari, Namibia) in *Affluence Without Abundance*:

> *The evidence of hunting and gathering societies suggests that both Marx and neoliberal economists were wrong about human nature: we are more than capable of leading fulfilled lives that are not defined by our labour. But if this is so, then why is it proving so hard for humans to embrace abundance the way hunter-gatherers did?*
>
> *In part it is because hunter-gatherers' 'primitive affluence' was neither a mind-set nor the economic expression of any particular ideology: there is no 'manifesto of primitive communism.' Their economic perspective was anchored in, among other things, their confidence in the providence of their environment, a hunter's empathy for his prey, an immediate-return economy, and indifference to the past and the future, and reaffirmed by social relationships shaped as much by jealousy as affection.*
>
> *It is also because there is another, more fundamental obstacle in the path to achieving Keynes's vision of technological advances and improved productivity ensuring that our absolute needs are being met with the minimum of effort. For the hunter-gatherer model of primitive affluence was not simply based on their having few needs easily satisfied; it also depended on no-one being substantially richer or more powerful than anyone else. If this kind of egalitarianism is a precondition for us to embrace a post-labour world, then I suspect it may prove to be a very hard nut to crack.*
>
> *Few Bushmen anywhere in southern Africa are able to easily*

meet their absolute needs today. In nutritional terms at least, most are worse off than they were as hunter-gatherers, plagued by the physical and social ailments we associate with poverty. And, of course, what they think of as their needs are now very different from what they were when they hunted and gathered.

But even among the few Ju|'hoansi at Skoonheid, Namibia, whose absolute needs are met with government welfare and who have been as surprised as they are pleased by recent developments at the resettlement camp, there is still a broader sense of dissatisfaction. And it is not only that they continue to endure the paternalism of others and are straitjacketed by their prejudices about Bushmen. It is because they consider the distribution of resources – most significantly land – to be grossly iniquitous. The jealously that once regulated Bushman band life has now been projected onto a broader canvas – one that reflects a much wider-lived reality that includes events and people who live beyond their immediate horizons.

Namibia has an exemplary record of governance since independence. There have been problems, but these have often been more a function of capacity and resources shortfalls rather than bad intentions. Yet Namibia, like its neighbours South Africa and Botswana, remains among the top five most unequal countries in the world. This inequality is not, as has so often been the case in the world's 'developing' economies, the result of the actions of a corrupt, kleptocratic class so much as a function of the nature of economic growth. But the net result is a massive concentration of available wealth in relatively few hands and a pronounced and obvious underclass making up half the population, with the Bushmen sitting at the bottom of the pile.

Even for those Ju|'hoansi at Skoonheid, inequality remains a burning issue, and one in which they find common cause with others in the bottom half of the economic pile everywhere else in the world. And if Ju|'hoansi are unable to accept a life of adequacy while others have much more, it suggests that Keynes may have put the cart before the horse. Perhaps the only way for us to embrace the abundance that has by and large already arrived is to find a way to deal with the inequality that inspires jealousy and anger as much as the impulse to work hard enough to keep up with or even overtake the Joneses (Suzman, 2017).

When a society generates wealth, there is an increase in absolute inequality (richest versus poorest) and an increase in relative inequality (the Gini or income shares) is also likely. Then, later in a modern economy, a theory goes that inequality should decline, tracing out an inverted U (the Kuznets curve) as social spending aims for some redistribution. However, international Gini curves (each country as a person) underestimate the inequality across the human race. After 1980, in the UK and the United States, inequality bounced back upwards during the electronic technology revolution, with globalisation allowing underbidding of wages and the eroding of social norms condemning conspicuous wealth. In his book, *Global Inequality: A New Approach for the Age of Globalisation*, Branko Milanovic (a senior scholar at the Luxembourg Income Study Centre) has defined two trends – declining inequality worldwide and increasing inequality within rich countries. The financial crisis of 2008 was really a recession in North Atlantic countries; less affected were the 'emerging global middling class', mainly in Asia. Globalisation helped the lower and middle classes of poor countries and the upper classes of rich countries much more than it helped the lower middle classes of rich countries (Milanovic, 2016).

Today, three quarters of the world's poorest people now live in middle-income countries because their nations have been reclassified as better off overall, but are simultaneously becoming more unequal. Ending human deprivation means tackling national distribution and international redistribution. The Kuznets curve suggests that as countries get richer, inequality must rise before it will eventually fall but this has been debunked, as actually it is indeed possible to achieve growth with equity. The problem, Thomas Piketty discovered, was that there were two types of household: those that own capital and those households that own only their own labour. 'Capitalism automatically generates arbitrary and unsustainable inequalities that radically undermine the meritocratic values on which democratic societies are based.' Memories of the Kuznets curve live on, lending credence to the myth of trickle-down economics.

Milanovic introduces the concept of Kuznets waves rather than a Kuznets curve. The twenty-first century's new rising inequality is a wave upstroke being driven by globalisation and technology. The two forces that will shape global inequality this century are economic convergence and Kuznets waves. World economic power will shift much more towards Asia. We cannot be sure that China is at the peak of its first Kuznets wave or the USA at the peak of its second Kuznets wave. Income inequality and political problems will remain closely linked and probably be accompanied by huge economic dislocation and a decline in the growth rate (Milanovic, 2016).

r > g = UBI

Furthermore, Piketty has clearly shown that the central contradiction of capitalism and its principal destabilising force is to do with the fact that the private rate of return on capital, r, typically 4% over the ages, can be significantly higher for long periods of time than the rate of growth of income (wages) and output, g, typically 1–1.5% historically.

The driver of inequality, the formula $r > g$, implies that wealth accumulated in the past grows more rapidly than output and wages. The past devours the future! The consequences for the long-term dynamics of wealth distribution are potentially terrifying, especially when one adds that the return on capital varies directly with the initial stake, perhaps acquired over 200 years ago in some cases. This non-egalitarian divergence in wealth distribution is occurring on a global scale (Piketty, 2014).

In the past, inequality has not been seen as an appropriate target for policy. However, perspectives on inequality have shifted dramatically as its systemically damaging effects – social, political, ecological and economic – have become all too clear, say Wilkinson and Pickett in *The Spirit Level* (2010). Much debate has occurred since as to whether more equal societies turn out to be healthier and happier.

Chris Hughes, the co-founder of Facebook, is well aware of this, and in his book *Fair Shot: Rethinking Inequality and How We Earn* introduces the new precariat – a hundred and fifty million Americans living from paycheck to paycheck, and it isn't because they aren't trying hard enough. Some might wonder – are they just not saving? Are they buying too many new gadgets and fancy cars when they should be diligently socking money away into a rainy day fund? Almost to a fault, every poor and middle-class person in these studies was attempting to build a nest egg. Nearly all the participants had savings accounts and many of them thought up ways to make it harder for them to touch the money. Lots of people have jobs but do not have any semblance of financial security in their lives. There is a reason that a reactionary US president leverages populist rhetoric at a time of record-low unemployment. We have the power to fix these problems by creating an income floor to support and stabilise the lives of poor and working-class Americans (Hughes, 2018).

Therefore, a universal basic income's promise should not be ignored. It could rationalise the patchwork of the hidden welfare state and it could smooth potential issues regarding robots replacing workers, allowing the workers to move to public jobs that markets won't support and robots can't do, or into meaningful volunteering (Pinker 2018). It could transform the life chances of the extreme poor in the Third World. UBI is not about equality of outcomes but rather equality of opportunity. Bregman also offers much support for a universal basic income. An experiment in London in May 2009, giving free money directly to homeless men, forced *The Economist* to conclude 'the most effective way to spend money on the homeless might be to give it to them' (Joseph Rowntree Foundation, 2010). It was thought 'free money makes people lazy', but according to the evidence, it doesn't – rather, free money works. In 2008, the government of Uganda decided to distribute almost $400 to some 12,000 sixteen to thirty-five year olds in return for a simple business plan. Five years later the results were staggering: incomes had gone up by nearly fifty per cent. Researchers from the University of Manchester summed up the benefits from similar programmes in their book *Just Give Money to the Poor* (2010): (1) households put money to good use; (2) poverty declines; (3) there can be diverse long-term benefits for income, health and tax revenues; and (4) the programmes cost less than the alternatives. A universal basic income has its proponents across the political spectrum. In 2009, Professor Forget, University of Manitoba, belatedly evaluated the data from the Mincome social experiment in Winnipeg, Canada and was surprised to find it was a resounding success. The data had been abandoned after a change in government, four years after the start of the project. In 1973, the provincial governor had chosen the small town of Dauphin and guaranteed a basic income, ensuring that no one fell below the poverty line. Over 1,000 families received the equivalent of £19,000, no questions asked. Birth rates dropped, school performance improved substantially, the 'Mincome cohort' studied harder, total hours worked reduced only slightly, hospitalisations decreased by 8.5% and impacts could be traced through to the next generation, both in earnings and health. A universal basic income nearly moved from experiment to law – but was finally shelved in the USA in 1978, after a statistical error suggested a jump in the number of divorces.

> *Can we revisit this castle in the sky or is it futile, dangerous and perverse? Even democracy seemed a glorious utopia not that long ago: Edmund Burke warned that democracy was futile (the masses were too foolish to handle it); dangerous (majority rule would be akin to playing with fire); and perverse (the 'general interest' would soon be corrupted by some crafty general). Compare this*

with the arguments against basic income. It's supposedly futile because we can't pay for it, dangerous because people would quit working, and perverse because ultimately a minority would end up having to toil harder to support the majority. But, for the first time in history we are actually rich enough to finance a sizeable basic income – therefore it is not futile. Certainly, some people may opt to work a bit less, but a basic income would free the poor from the welfare trap and spur them to seek a paid job with true opportunities for growth and advancement – therefore it is not dangerous. The welfare state, in many places, has degenerated into a system of suspicion and shame. In terms of redistribution, a basic income would meet the political left's demands for fairness and it would give the political right a more limited government – therefore it is not perverse (Bregman, 2018).

Back in 2005, the economist Jeffrey Sachs, in his book *The End of Poverty,* acknowledged that the extreme poor were completely unable to get onto the bottom rung of the development ladder no matter how hard they tried! They were never able to save any of their meagre annual income because they were fighting daily against starvation, disease and death. Sachs' main suggestion was for all the developed nations to reach a 0.7% of GDP target for Official Development Assistance (ODA). Even at 2005 values, this is not nearly adequate enough, especially if now climate change amelioration and reparations for the colonial past have to be factored in. A universal basic income set at $5,000 would cost $30 trillion (6 billion humans above infancy x $5,000). This would provide both a leg up for individuals and a tax base for governments to develop national and local infrastructure.

How do you raise $30 trillion? Well, a good place to go looking would be among those with some money. The Pareto distribution can help in this regard (see appendix 2).

In the United States the wealth breakdown is approximately given by the following table:

Percentile Fraction of the Population	Per Cent of Wealth Held
Upper 1%	34.3%
95%–99%	24.6%
90%–95%	12.3%

80%–90%	13.4%
60%–80%	11.3%
40%–60%	3.8%
0%–40%	0.02%

A <u>global</u> wealth pyramid shows similar data in a different way:

Figure 1: The global wealth pyramid 2018

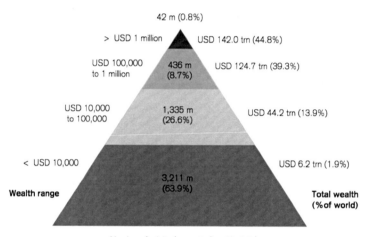

Number of adults (percent of world adults)

If we plot the Pareto graph for the current unequal situation worldwide, we could set the area under the curve to estimate a tax take of $30 trillion. (see appendix 2). If the total global net assets are approximately $240 trillion, we are looking to raise 12.5% for a universal basic income fund. To raise that money we need to divide the top of the pyramid up into various segments of different tax rates. It is very important to remember that we are aiming to tax wealth <u>not</u> income here. It will remain up to sovereign governments to run their own tax policies on income.

Firstly, the **Ultra High-Net-Worth Individuals** are those with wealth assets of greater than $30 million. There were over 200,000 such individuals in 2013.

	Net Assets each $ million	No of individuals	Total Wealth $bn	Global Wealth Tax rate	Tax Take $bn
	>1 billion	2,170	6,516	60%	3,909
	550–999	1,080	929	55%	511
	500–549	2,660	1,695	50%	847
	250–499	8,695	3,420	45%	1,539
	200–249	14,185	3,205	40%	1,282
	100–199	23,835	3,780	35%	1,323
	50–99	60,760	4,720	30%	1,416
	30–49	85,850	3,505	25%	876
Totals	approx.	200,000	$27 tn		$11.7 tn

(The World Ultra Wealth Report, 2017)

High-Net-Worth Individuals can be defined as having net assets between $1 million and $30 million. In 2016 there were 16.5 million such individuals worldwide, with a total net wealth of $63.5 trillion. If the average tax take was set at 22% (actually varying within the range 5%–24%) perhaps $14 trillion would be raised. (The Economist, 2017).

The third segment of the population who are of interest are the 'mass affluent' – net assets of $100,000 to $1 million. There are roughly 600 million such individuals (the rest of the top ten per cent of the wealth pyramid) with total net assets of $101 trillion. Using a tax rate here of say 5%, the tax take would be approximately $5.4 trillion (Wikipedia, 2018).

So we end up with a Global Progressive Wealth Tax Income in year one as shown:

$11.7 tn + $14.0 tn + $5.4 tn = $31.1 trillion

Obviously these are estimated figures and if redistributed as a universal basic income this money would at once reduce inequality to such an extent as to require a different Pareto curve in year two with a lower 'n' value (see appendix 2) and a wider tax base (perhaps the top fifteen per cent of the wealth pyramid).

However, there are problems with a Global Progressive Wealth Tax precisely because it is trying to tax wealth. The issue of valuation is tricky.

Determining a rich person's precise net wealth is difficult, even for the wealthy themselves. Perhaps sixty per cent of the wealth of the top one per cent is 'non-financial' – vehicles, boats, real estate and, most difficult of all, private businesses. Also, as soon as the tax rate rises above the rate of return on capital (approximately four per cent), the wealthy can no longer pay the tax out of income interest on their capital. It starts to bite into their capital. This is the whole point of some redistribution. But just how do the wealthy liquidate assets to pay more tax? It may be possible to sell some stocks and shares to the pension funds, but after that how can valuable properties or businesses be sold if all other members of the wealthy classes are trying to do the same? Just who is going to buy? (Worstall, 2014).

So in the real world it would be difficult to impose a wealth tax above twenty per cent on any of the ultra high-net-worth individuals because of the issues of valuation and liquidity. This means that the total tax take in year one will probably be about half of the example above ($5 trillion). As a consequence the total tax take might only be $25 trillion, therefore allowing an annual universal basic income of $4,100 approximately.

Globalisation is eroding the wages of the lower and middle classes and the robot revolution could remove middle-class jobs altogether, so never before has the time been so ripe for the introduction of a universal, unconditional basic income. The Land of Plenty is rich thanks to the institutions, the knowledge and the social capital amassed for us by our forebears. This wealth belongs to us all (Bregman, 2018).

In 1940s Britain, Lady Juliet Rhys-Williams developed the idea of the 'negative income tax', which became the most popular design for how to create a guaranteed income for most of the twentieth century. She proposed a cash allowance delivered through the tax system, increasing the further below the poverty line a person falls.

To be clear, Hughes is not proposing a <u>universal</u> basic income. Proponents of a US-based UBI, like Bregman, favour giving every American, regardless of their wealth or whether they work, $1,000 per month (that is triple the worked example shown above, which is globally focused and my preferred option) with no strings attached. A guaranteed income for working people in Hughes' mind, by contrast, would go to a more narrow set of recipients, specifically working people in need, and would cost much less. A guaranteed income designed in this particular way – $500 a month to working people making under $50,000 per year – would be a most powerful tool to combat inequality in the country. And it would encourage work by making it pay (Hughes, 2018).

Optimism and pessimism have become synonymous with consumer confidence or the lack thereof. Radical ideas about the world have almost literally become unthinkable. Politics has been watered down to problem management. Right separates from left on a percentage point or two of the income tax rate. Journalism portrays politics as a game in which the stakes are not ideas, but careers (Bregman, 2018). All these issues seem to loom large if viewed from inside the bubble of the developed world.

Worldviews

Internationally, not all is negative and some progress is being made – worldwide measles cases are falling and fertility rates are decreasing. Yet, in 2012, over 1,100 children under five died every day because extreme poverty inevitably leads to hunger, illiteracy, disease, brain damage and death. Poverty's complex causes are many – poor personal choices, unethical worldviews of some religions, natural disasters, lack of knowledge/technology, great inequalities of power and even the residual effects of Western colonialism (Sider, 2015). Of course, these views are challenged. David Chilton (Reformed Pastor, Placerville, California), in particular, took issue with anything he felt advocated socialism or 'statism' in his provocative book *Productive Christians in an Age of Guilt Manipulators*. He was an advocate of extreme liberalism and felt Ron Sider, the Canadian theologian and Christian activist, had substituted his own 'Marxist Manifesto of social justice' instead of the principles outlined in the book of Deuteronomy. The neoliberal Chilton believed the Bible allows for slavery and Sider was wrong to condemn it! Rather, economic power in the hands of private individuals is *never* complete power over the whole life of a poor person whereas centralised state power, he felt, creates dependence scarcely distinguishable from complete slavery (Chilton, 1981).

The Atlantic Slave Trade in the eighteenth century was a source of high profits for some yet was a great evil and is certainly seen as such from our vantage point in the twenty-first century. But, one wonders, will future generations look at the grossly unfair economic conditions of our age as an equally great evil? What would Fredrick Douglass, the nineteenth-century African-American abolitionist and social reformer, have to say about today's inequality? Current economic conditions, which effectively remove all hope of under-developed nations ever being able to emerge out from under crushing debts, are morally unacceptable because they hold back infrastructure and sustainable development in the Third World. A totally restructured global economy and financial system combining more assistance, in the form of grants, with more diligence on the part of lenders will make it less likely that so many of the poorest countries in the world will, in the future, be burdened with excessive debt and will therefore be able to improve their basic infrastructure (Stiglitz, 2006).

Take water as a simple example. In the Land of Plenty, we are very fortunate to have clean, safe water available to us whenever we need it. We simply turn the tap on and out it comes. We flush the toilet and water takes our waste away. In some of the world's poorest communities, women and children have to get up at dawn and walk for miles to collect water for their families. There are no taps with safe clean water in their homes or even near their homes to use. They have to go to lakes, ponds, streams and rivers to fetch water. There is often nowhere safe or private to go to the toilet. Around 650 million people have no choice but to drink dirty water. 2.3 billion people don't have access to a proper toilet. As a result, over 500,000 children a year, or 1,400 a day, still die from diarrhoea caused by unsafe water and poor toilets, but it doesn't have to be this way.

Understandably charities want to respond to urgent need. *WaterAid* is an admirable international charity, working in thirty-seven countries across the world to transform lives by improving access to safe water and improving hygiene and toilets in the world's poorest communities. They have helped to deliver safe water to 1.9 million people during 2017 and toilets to 2.9 million people, as well as delivering lifesaving hygiene education to an estimated 4.1 million people. *WaterAid* wants everyone, everywhere to have access to safe water and sanitation by 2030. Without safe water or toilets, people are trapped in a cycle of poverty and disease. Many of the problems in meeting debt payments arise not from mistakes on the part of developing countries but from the instabilities of the global economic and financial systems. The need for better mechanisms for sharing risk and for solving debt problems will continue to be great so long as international financial markets continue to be marked by instability (Stiglitz, 2006).

Even in the Land of Plenty, unfair economic conditions lead to much inequality and, although there is not the extreme poverty of the Third World, there is much discontent. The poor borrow more, save less, smoke more, exercise less, drink more, and eat less healthfully. Offer money management training and the poor are the last to sign up. They often write the worst job applications and show up at interviews in the least professional attire. People behave differently when they believe a thing to be scarce – a 'scarcity mentality' – and are good at managing short-term problems but the long-term perspective goes out the window. Scarcity, whether of time or of money, leads to unwise decisions. You can't take a break from poverty; it simply compromises your mental bandwidth or calmness of mind to make good choices and decisions. Greg Duncan, a professor at the University of California, calculated that lifting an American family out of poverty takes an average of about $4,500 annually, but would pay for itself by the time the poor children reached middle age. (Duncan, 2008). The very poor, those whose bandwidth is already overtaxed and whose needs are greatest, are the least likely to seek help. Nudges are hugely popular with politicians in our modern Land of Plenty because they cost next to nothing. Nudges might help combat the symptoms of poverty slightly, but they solve nothing in the long run. As long as inequality continues to rise, the gross domestic mental bandwidth will continue to contract.

Whether you look at the incidences of depression, burnout, drug abuse, high dropout rates, obesity, unhappy childhoods, low election turnout, or social and political distrust, the evidence points to the same culprit every time: inequality. Shouldn't we be more concerned with equal opportunities than with equal wealth? They both matter. When inequality goes up, social mobility goes down. There is almost no country on earth where the American Dream is less likely than the USA. Society cannot function without some degree of inequality but marked income inequality makes us all less happy with our lives, even if we are relatively well off. If you are poor, your main problem is no money; if you are homeless, your main problem is no roof over your head. In Europe, the number of vacant houses is double the number of homeless. So the Dutch, in 2006, provided free housing to get everyone off the street, instead of the police chasing vagrants, and doctors/social workers applying 'Band-Aid' solutions. It was a great success until the financial crisis (Bregman, 2018).

There are many reasons to tackle inequality. If we reduce inequality of economic outcomes, then this contributes to securing the equality of opportunity that is seen as a key feature of a modern democratic society. Social evils, such as crime and ill health, are attributed to the highly unequal nature of societies today. These provide an instrumental reason for seeking to achieve lower levels of poverty and inequality, as does the fear that extremes of inequality are incompatible with a functioning democracy. The present levels of economic inequality are intrinsically inconsistent with the conception of a good society. Atkinson asked in 2015: 'If we wish to reduce the extent of inequality, how can this be done?' This is not really an exercise in utopianism. Rather, it indicates directions of movement for those concerned with reducing inequality and it starts with the current state of society. The steps to be taken depend on the reasons that societies are so unequal and why inequality has risen in recent decades. There is a need to place distributional issues at the heart of the analysis. This is not a fashionable position among economists, but one that is essential; not only to provide an understanding of inequality but also to explain the workings of economies and to tackle the major policy challenges facing us today. It makes little sense to propose that the world consists of similar people with the same interests if we are confronting problems of restoring fiscal balance, of ageing populations, of climate change or of international imbalances. Consideration of the distributional dimensions is necessary if we are to relate the big numbers of economic policy to the real-life experience of individual citizens. We cannot escape from $r > g$!

Atkinson felt that we need to understand how societies developed in the past, especially in terms of episodes of time during which inequality fell rather than just long-run trends. He was sure inequality was lessened by changes in markets (both capital and labour) and was not just a matter of an increased premium on educational qualifications. The world is changing in significant respects, notably in the nature of employment and in the relation between wealth (as a source of income) and capital (as a source of control) (Atkinson, 2015).

Internationally, hundreds of millions of people still have to survive on about a dollar and a half a day. The whole world needs to encourage these nations to catch up in terms of economic development *in a sustainable way*. To allow their natural resources to be harnessed for the benefit of their whole populations rather than used to pay off international debts! They must be given the chance to be able to use their resources in a more sustainable way and be therefore more resilient as the world faces an *uncertain* future.

A recent report in 2012, *Share the World's Resources*, finds that at least $400 billion of debt in one hundred different countries needs to be cancelled simply so that states can have enough money to meet the basic needs of their citizens. One approach would be to cancel 'dictator debts'. Dictator debts presently amount to about $735 billion in thirty-two different countries. Citizens never agreed to these loans and never benefitted from them. These types of debt cancellations would mean the World Bank relinquishing their authority over debtor countries (Hickel, 2017).

Human nature

At this point it would be helpful to draw aside for a moment and consider the related issues of human nature, self-centredness and greed. Mark Cocker has brilliantly exposed historical greed, on the part of previous generations of Europeans, in his book *Rivers of Blood, Rivers of Gold*. In great detail, he elucidates how different groups of Europeans, in their lust for power, wealth and resources, laid to waste different tribal peoples. The Spanish, in Central America in the sixteenth century, in their quest for gold, destroyed the Mexica (Aztec) 'civilisation'. The British, in Tasmania in the nineteenth century, colonising the island, brought about the extinction of the Aboriginal people and replaced them with sheep. In a similar fashion, the Euro-American white population's drive westwards in North America for more and more territory abolished the Apache (and all other Native Americans') way of life. And finally Cocker explains how the Germans in South West Africa attempted genocide with much cruelty and brutality. The Nama and the Herero lost between half and three quarters of their total numbers. A total of about 75,000 African inhabitants perished due to disease or war between 1904 and 1907. The remnants were reduced to a landless proletariat, ground under by one of the most oppressive colonial regimes. Of course, it is a fact that tribal peoples were often capable of behaviour just as brutal as those inflicted upon them by their European conquerors. In ancient Mexico, there was regular offering of human life to American gods. We need also to acknowledge Apache excesses, which were abominable and militarily pointless. But so often in European terms, technological inferiority equalled moral inferiority and, at times, moral worthlessness. The effects of subsequent asset stripping rolled down through the centuries. In Latin America today, Guatemala still has a poor land distribution record, with ninety-eight per cent of the Mayan population either landless or with insufficient land to support themselves (Cocker, 1999).

So what aspects of human nature must we try and leave behind to live in a better world? In Mark 10:13–30, Jesus suggests, in this instance, that resistance to the generosity of the Kingdom of God is the typical attitude of the adult. In contrast, we need to reawaken the qualities that are characteristic of childhood. Children are open, receptive, grateful and therefore less greedy. In his response to the rich man, Jesus puts justice before piety, teaching the need to distribute wealth more fairly rather than simply staying on the right side of the law (Faller, 2018).

Are modern Europeans capable of learning from the more distant past as well as from their recent experiences of two world wars? A good case can be made for the European Union maintaining peace in Europe for the last seventy years – but what about the effects its greed has on the rest of the world, particularly the descendants of the tribal peoples treated so badly in previous centuries? Perhaps modern economies need to be embedded in such a way to make some reparation for the past and thereby belatedly restore some equity across the human race.

Reflecting on other aspects of human nature, Vishvapani, a Welsh Buddhist theologian, on BBC Radio 4 in January 2019, suggested the need to create cultures for lasting change:

> *Global warming was on the agenda at Davos with naturalist David Attenborough, and a Swedish 15-year-old, Greta Thunberg, who has inspired teenagers across the world. She recently told the UN Conference on Climate Change: 'You say that you love your children above all else yet you are stealing their future in front of their very eyes'.*
>
> *In Wales, these protests resonate with a piece of legislation that deserves to be better known. The 'Well-being of Future Generations Act 2015' states that for the future of our children every public body in Wales must operate according to sustainable development principles. Reducing carbon emissions is just the start. The Act states policy makers must think long-term, work collaboratively and involve ordinary people in their decisions. Every government action must take account of the need to create a more prosperous and healthy society with a thriving culture because the well-being of humanity as a whole cannot be separated from the well-being of individuals and communities. And all this means fundamentally challenging how government operates.*
>
> *It is challenging to implement at every level. But it resonates with Buddhism which acknowledges that human beings typically are driven by unconscious emotions and the focus on short-term gains at the cost of our long-term interests. Everyone wants to be happy; but when we look for happiness in immediate pleasures of prioritising our own interests over others, we turn happiness into an objective that we can grasp. However, Buddhism suggests that the grasping mentality is itself an important part of what makes us unhappy. If it is true of individuals, it is also true of society; in either case, the alternative is fostering the altruistic conditions that support our long-term well-being.*
>
> *Greta Thunberg, the Swedish teenager, is admirably impatient*

and rightly burdened that we recognise climate change as a crisis that requires urgent action. But acting in ways that are effective in the long-term means recognising that we need to think <u>freshly</u> and think <u>big</u>. Perhaps we can't easily change human nature but what is happening in Wales shows that at least we can reconceive our activities in a considered way, even at the level of a government, to create the cultures for lasting change (Vishvapani, 2019).

Perhaps the European Union has had its day, and it is now time to move on, think big and become more inclusive. Supranational institutions need to be carefully designed, bearing in mind the mistakes of the past, to focus on combating inequality and climate change at every turn. We will return to this in more detail in Chapter 7 and subsequent chapters.

Debt

In 1967, the Arab–Israeli Six Day War eventually led to the Oil Crisis in the 1970s. OPEC states found themselves awash with petrodollars which poured into US banks. So the banks invested the money abroad in the form of loans to the Global South to build their economies. This was considered to be a safe investment. The loan pushers gave little thought to whether the recipients would ever be able to pay them back. Debt levels in the Global South eventually skyrocketed via the mechanism of compound interest. Mexico, Brazil and Argentina defaulted in the Third World Debt Crisis – a catastrophe for the bankers. The US government had to bail them out and the IMF stepped in with structural adjustment programmes (SAPs) to manage the Global South's debt repayment. SAPs introduced austerity, privatisation and liberalisation. The promise was to grow out of debt but spending cuts were funnelling monies back to Wall Street, and poor countries opening their markets to globalisation and foreign direct investment sucked money to the global elite. SAPs were imposed not by violent coups but by leveraging debt – the end result was loss of national sovereignty.

The IMF and the World Bank promised the world that structural adjustment would improve economic growth and reduce poverty, but it simply reversed all the gains made during the development period. The 'IMF riots' during the 1980s were the predictable result, but they had little effect. The IMF and the World Bank have immunity status under the International Organisations Immunity Act of 1945 and have voting power allocated in favour of the G7. So, all of the risks associated with SAPs belong to the debtor countries. Criticism of this has come from Joseph Stiglitz (World Bank economist) and

Davison Budhoo (IMF economist). Since 2000, the IMF and the World Bank now allow a bit more room for social spending.

The race to the bottom triggered by the debt system, structural adjustment and globalisation is one of the main drivers of inequality. Economic and political freedom has been attacked in the name of economic and political freedom by unfair uncontrolled neoliberal systems (Hickel, 2017). It is time to search for a new economic system.

The Foundational Economy
Manchester Capital (part of the Centre for Research on Socio-Cultural Change at Manchester University) suggests a foundational economy would be dependent on the discharge of social obligations in the form of sourcing, training and living wages. They contend that the British economy has been a laboratory of experimentation for the past century. They narrow their focus to the post-1945 period and concentrate on two thirty-year policy experiments – the post-war settlement (the welfare state) and the post-1979 experiment (Thatcher–Blair).

But current capitalism is not working well. Corporate business is about point value and passing risk, while avoiding social responsibility and the obligation to provide reasonable quality, sustainable, everyday economic services at accessible prices. Three sectoral cases (telecoms/broadband, supermarkets/dairy and retail banking) were examined to make the case for social licensing.

Privatisation of fixed-line telecoms in the UK has delivered a system in which the private and public interests are only partially aligned in relation to the provision of broadband. In a few years' time, the UK may well be left with an inadequate fibre infrastructure, which nonetheless generates huge amounts of cash for BT shareholders.

The intense competition between milk processors in a vertically-disintegrated supply chain is economically efficient from the perspective of week-by-week point value calculations of supermarket consumers. But on an industry-wide level it leads to problems regarding capacity underutilisation and necessitates opportunist short-termism on the part of the processors, which can have adverse consequences for wages and the environment.

Retail banking needs to recognise that mis-selling is the nearly inevitable result of ambitious return on equity (RoE) targets. The starting point in reform has to be a new business model which combines two key features: first, much lower RoE targets of less than ten per cent, and second, charging bank fees on some declared basis to recover the costs of current account and other basic services. Retail banking is the prime case for social licensing, probably on a regional basis, to prevent property price bubbles.

In introducing their *Foundational Economy* concept these researchers at the Centre for Research on Socio-Cultural Change (cresc.ac.uk) contrast the views of Boris Johnson with those of Fernand Braudel:

> *Like it or not, the free market economy is the only show in town. Britain is competing in an increasingly impatient and globalised economy, in which competition is getting ever stiffer.*
> Boris Johnston MP, Margaret Thatcher Lecture (2013)

> *There were not one but several economies.*
> Fernand Braudel, The Structures of Everyday Life (1981)

As a corrective to the Boris Johnson-like framing, Braudel's idea of several distinct spheres of economic life can include a *foundational economy* – an infra-economy producing mundane goods and services which is beneath notice most of the time. Another insight is that modern capitalism is not only about the establishment of a free competitive market but also about entrenching an anti-market system in which the state is the guarantor of a profitable monopoly that benefits a few. Such sectors should be placed under an explicit obligation to meet specified economic and social objectives – an argument for experiments with social licensing.

The *foundational economy* is the economic zone that produces goods and services which, firstly, are necessary for everyday life; secondly, which are consumed by all citizens regardless of income; and thirdly, which are therefore distributed according to population through branches and networks.

Firms and sectors will need to change to secure long-term sustainability and resilience within a foundational economy capable of delivering high quality and accessible economic and social services. The current private and public sector business models will have to be challenged to experiment with social licences. For example, in the foundational economy, as in countries sitting on large mineral deposits, businesses need to earn the right to extract cash from a territory rather than expect sweeteners to operate locally.

How can we lever change? Well, in Britain, for example, the state needs to be decentralised. All the necessary social licensing experiments cannot take place in a single location or within a single framework. A truly experimental form of social licensing within a learning state will need powerful and substantially autonomous elected authorities, and will cultivate forms of cognitive modesty abandoning 'one size fits all' (Bowman, 2014).

Such a Foundational Embedded Economy aims to end the myth of the self-contained, self-sustaining market, replacing it with provisioning by the household, market, commons and state. An understanding of the many distinct sources of wealth – natural, social, human, physical and financial – on which our well-being depends is something we all need to factor into our thinking. Rather than focusing by default on how to increase economic activity, we should ask how the content and structure of that activity might be shaping society, politics and power to address inequality and then ask just how big can the economy become, given Earth's ecological capacity (Raworth, 2017)? In the end, inequality can only sensibly be addressed if human beings embrace again the concept of limits.

CHAPTER 4

LIMITS

PEOPLE ACROSS THE WORLD and at all levels of society need to accept limits in all things. Modern governments adopt a default position of chasing after more and more growth to finance their spending on welfare, health, education or housing in order to fulfil their promises and satisfy the ambitions of their populations. If the growth is not as strong as expected then government deficits enlarge.

All hyper-inflations are caused by the excessive printing of money to finance government deficits that have been allowed to spiral out of control (King, 2016). Printing money to finance projects is always couched in terms such as 'investing in the nation's future'. Money itself is not bad. God expects people to be productive and provide for themselves. There is nothing ungodly about a profit margin – it is the expected result of hard work sincerely done. However, Western culture is rampantly consumerist and it is wrong to swim unthinkingly along in that stream. The answer is not to join a commune or to live on the street. We should live radically differently to our whole current culture but also live within it (Beynon, 2011) and try and change it from within. Here, Raworth would agree – stating her **third idea** of nurturing human nature away from rational economic man towards more social, adaptable human beings.

WEIRD

Throughout the twentieth century, widespread use of the word 'consumer' grew steadily in public life, policymaking and the media until it far outstripped the word 'citizen'. Consumers find expression only in the market place. Raworth wants the twenty-first century to be different. It could be pointed out that rational economic man is a fallacy when faced with powerful advertising and mis/disinformation.

Rather than narrowly self-interested, we are to be social and reciprocating.

Generally people like cooperating, especially if others reciprocate. But people are also ready to punish free riders even if it costs to do so. The degree to which people become self-interested varies across different societies and, to a certain extent, depends on the state's provisioning for society's needs. In the UK, a new Universal Credit system has been introduced ostensibly to encourage people back into work. There may also be an element of making it more difficult to abuse the benefits system, which had become increasingly complicated. On a more positive and reciprocating note, the charity and voluntary sectors are strong in the UK.

Instead of being isolated we are to be interdependent.
Going with the crowd is a common phenomenon. This will only become more prevalent in the future as lives become more tightly networked. Worldwide communications now mean we live in an emerging dynamic global network-of- networks (Ormerod, 1999). Initiatives to encourage change in behaviour can be difficult to predict. Tax on sugar or discounts on solar panels often fail to achieve their expected results, leaving economists and social planners disappointed. Much more effective have been taxes on leaded petrol and plastic bags. There is much yet to be done to convince populations that we all need to be interdependent (both developed world and developing worlds).

Rather than calculate, we usually approximate.
Biases are the underpinnings of our heuristics, the unconscious mental shortcuts we take every time we use a 'rule of thumb' to make decisions. In many contexts those heuristics lead us to make better decisions than exact calculations would do. Raworth gives the example of coronary care from Gigerenzer's work: doctors asking three simple questions based on the electrocardiogram, chest pain and other symptoms out-performed a complex computer programme in diagnostic accuracy. But change that is invisible, delayed, gradual and distant has the very characteristics that our heuristic decision tools are infamously bad at handling well. And this is the very change that is occurring to the planet's ecosystems. So the smart way forward encourages a judicious mix of risk-savvy heuristics and behavioural nudges.

Far from having dominion over nature, we are deeply embedded in the web of life.
Man's seeming dominion over nature runs far back in Western culture, at least to the Bible's opening verses. But thoughtful environmentalists are continually stressing that humanity is actually embedded <u>within</u> nature. This

is obviously a difficult concept for children growing up in Western urban centres to comprehend. Children from rural Third World communities will have a far less simplistic and anthropomorphic understanding of the living world.

This portrait most closely illustrates the shifts that people in WEIRD societies (Western, Educated, Industrialised, Rich and Democratic) must make. Some would add an extra 'D' for denial. As we face these existential threats, we live, unfortunately, in an age of denial. How can the insights be shifted in ways that can help to bring all of humanity into the Doughnut? The growing use of monetary incentives in policies is aimed at ending human deprivation and ecological degradation. But there may be far wiser ways – drawing on what we now know about values, nudges, networks and reciprocity – to nurture human nature towards the Doughnut's safe and just space (Raworth, 2017).

Wendell Berry knows we need far wiser ways. Writing back in 2006, he asked:

> …*Will we keep on consuming, spending, wasting and driving around at any cost to anything and everybody but ourselves? Will science find an answer to prove that our modern way of life is indestructible? To believe yes was always indefensible and now looks manifestly foolish. But foolishness on this scale looks disturbingly like a sort of international insanity. The real names of global warming are 'waste' and 'greed'. We seem to have come to a collective delusion of grandeur, insisting that all of us are 'free' to be as conspicuously greedy and wasteful as the most corrupt of kings and queens ever were. The problem is not only prodigal extravagance, but also an assumed godly limitlessness. The United States has 250 billion tons of recoverable coal reserves – enough to last 100 years even at double the current rate of consumption (in 2006). The world-ending fire of industrial fundamentalism may already be burning in our furnaces and engines. Surely it would be better to intend straightforwardly to contain the fire and eventually put it out? Until now this supposed economy has no plan for temperance or thrift or the ecological law of return. It will do anything. It is monstrous by definition (Berry, 2006).*

So it is going to be very difficult for WEIRD societies to change. But at least the alchemy of money creation must be challenged – challenged vigorously and challenged soon. Putting all our trust in money is foolish. There are ethical questions of great importance in many of today's societies in relation to greed. The normal expectation, of certainly the last twenty years or more, of everyone rising up the escalator of wealth needs to be morally challenged. The rampant individualism that drives UK university vice-chancellors' pay levels to over three times that of the Prime Minister, while students take on more and more debt while at university, must be challenged as a complete loss of balance and clearly stepping outside morally acceptable limits. As stated before, the argument for trickle-down economics is weak. More fundamentally, it is time to challenge the notion that we comfortable Westerners can assume our comfort and 'standard of living' can continue. It is more convincing to believe that there has to be a downward dip in the West's standard of living, not just a catch-up by non-Western peoples. There can be no pain-free transition for those of us in the West who have gotten used to those comforts. It probably means having colder homes in winter, forswearing red meat, using very little air travel and much less private transport (imagine the school run without the car!)

Work, leisure and money

> Stable and meaningful work plays a crucial part in every life well lived. But no matter how important work is in our lives, many yearn for a shorter workweek. Working less provides bandwidth for other things, like family, community involvement and recreation. We cannot all just go ahead and switch to a 15–30 hour workweek. Reduction of work first has to be reinstated as a political idea – trading money for time. It all starts with reversing incentives. Currently, it is cheaper for employers to have one person work overtime than hire two part-time. We need to invest more in education, develop a more flexible retirement system and make good provisions for paternity leave and childcare.
>
> In overworked countries, people watch an absurd amount of television – up to five hours a day in the US. True leisure, however, is neither a luxury nor a vice. It is vital to our brains and our bodies. A twenty-first century education should prepare people not only for joining the workforce but also for life. We can handle the good life, if only we take the time (Bregman, 2018).

A sensible amount of work to earn money for today's needs and to make some provision for the future is fine. There is nothing wrong with money and what it can buy. The trouble is that there is something wrong with people. That is where the danger starts. Money is dangerous because it is not simply a matter of advice and decision-making; it is not just about budgets, careful spending, and wise investments. It is about people's hearts. This is why the love of money is the root of all kinds of evil (1 Timothy 6:10). And none of us are immune; from poverty to wealth and everywhere in between, love of money is pervasive (Beynon, 2011).

Money can be used well, especially for the well-being of others. We do not need to be negative about money. We can use our money in good and meaningful ways. A caring society needs to put limits on greed and individualism but not on the well-being of others. This is deeply unsettling. But WEIRD societies need limits and they need to change. We would be better advised to put our trust in God's blueprint for our lives and our actions. The blueprint is outlined by Craig Blomberg, Professor of the New Testament at Denver Seminary, Colorado, in *Neither Poverty nor Riches* (1999). From the Old Testament, Blomberg suggests:

- 'Extreme wealth and extreme poverty both appear undesirable.'
- 'We must seek neither poverty nor riches. Those who have already been blessed with wealth must be generous and compassionate in using it.'
- 'The key to evaluating any individual church or nation in terms of its use of material possessions ... is how well it takes care of the poor and powerless in its midst ...'
- '... Judaism had a God who cared passionately about the poor and marginalized and opposed both religious idolatry and social injustice.'

In application of the New Testament precedent for holistic ministry, Blomberg argues that Christians are to meet physical needs, while at the same time explaining that only God can completely and ultimately rescue one from both temporal and eternal plights (Blomberg, 1999). Then it will be easier to enter the Doughnut's safe and just space.

No one can accurately predict the future. But the alchemy of money creation fosters the illusion of unbounded pleasure and the temptation to issue so much money and take on so much debt in good times that the result is not prosperity but rising inflation, leading to economic chaos and the destruction of well-being (King, 2016). Money can become god; a deity that is loved and served. Money is deceptive and draws us to worship it and depend on it, rather than God.

There are two main lies which the money-god peddles to us. The first is this: money offers us life now. We are greedy for more money because we believe that instinctive feeling that at some level life consists of what we have.

The second is this: money offers us security for the future. We so easily think we are safe because of money in the bank, house ownership, or a good pension plan. This ignores what Mervyn King calls 'radical uncertainty'. We know we should not put our hope in money but our culture seems to believe insurance is the answer for many financial problems – whether insurance for your life, your health or your television! Something is wrong with the heart when confidence and peace flow from our insurance policies rather than from a loving Heavenly Father (Beynon, 2011).

Limitlessness

Of course, both Berry and Kingsnorth, just like Raworth, wish to implore everyone towards the need for limits, rather than a never-ending hankering after growth. The commonly accepted basis of our present economy is the fantastical possibility of limitless growth, limitless wants, limitless wealth, limitless natural resources, and limitless debt. In this doctrine all are entitled to pursue without limit whatever they conceive as desirable. This results in the minimisation of neighbourliness, respect, reverence, responsibility, accountability and self-subordination (Berry, 2017).

It is worth taking time to ponder the results of the loss of these qualities in modern Western society. It seems that the quest to 'keep up' in the midst of a materialistic, consumerist society leads to much unhappiness. Even Pinker admits that Americans have become unhappier, despite the benefits showered on them. He recognises, of course, that some people find a life of mere material welfare empty and mourn the deeper sense of purpose that religious faith gave. The use of anti-depressants has expanded to levels in the ordinary population never seen before. There are also huge amounts of prescription opiates being used leading to widespread addictions. This is happening in an era when people are actually living healthier and longer lives. What is going on? Is it that folk cannot apply sensible boundaries to their lives and therefore cannot find contentment in having what is sufficient as opposed to looking enviously around at what others have? The Reverend George Preston, Presbyterian Minister, addressed this issue in a 2009 sermon on Psalm 34, when he drew a distinction between happiness (often dependent on happenings and circumstances) and Christian joy (not dependent on circumstances – 2 Corinthians 7:4). If only some of Psalm 34 and these eternal lessons had been taken to heart in middle America, the sub-prime mortgage explosion, facilitated by complex derivatives set up by the banks, might have been avoided. What a blessing that would have been for the whole world!

King admits borrowing short to lend long creates risk and no more so than when new financial instruments so created (derivatives) are traded largely among big financial institutions allowing those rich and super-rich (the top ten per cent) with sufficient capital to take risks and become even wealthier. Thus, the financial system has become enormously interconnected and complex (King, 2016). And such complicated loans became extremely dangerous in the mid 2000s, especially to the ninety per cent. Neil Alldred, Lecturer in Politics, Belfast Metropolitan College, (in reply to Financial Times: December 17, 2015 *European stocks bounce off 10-week lows*) feels 'Popular capitalism wasn't meant to work like this' – unhelpful advice from independent financial advisers is not merely inaccurate but downright harmful. He cites Joseph Stiglitz earning his Nobel Prize for economics by investigating the lack of information available to actors in market situations (Alldred, 2015).

There is such a thing as a responsible budgeted loan, a mortgage to buy a house for example, but there are real dangers involved. Paying interest on the loan ends up costing more – a foolish way of spending. Our culture will encourage us to have items now, which we cannot afford – 'buy now, pay later' has become the mantra of today. Previous generations would have waited and saved before making a purchase for something that they really needed. Credit cards have a high interest rate but a low minimum monthly repayment to encourage lots of interest. It has now become culturally normal to be in debt! (Beynon, 2011). This is not just a problem for individual citizens – governments are equally guilty.

The people of sub-Saharan Africa are probably not that concerned with inequality between the social class groups that occur within the UK, however wide it may now be. But they may look at the £1.7 trillion UK debt on the government 'credit card' and wonder how it can be fair that this is used to fund a welfare state provision which they can only dream of. This state of affairs is morally bankrupt. But not many are suggesting that it is time each individual in the UK started to pay to the Chancellor of the Exchequer the £26,000 that they 'owe' him! (Debt £1.7 trillion / 60 million population = £26,000 each approximately.) The Chancellor has no money of his own to pay off the national debt. He needs to get his hands into the wallets of those who have wealth and savings. These folk are a relatively small segment of the population because the average household debt in the UK has doubled in the last decade. Everyone is encouraged to spend by borrowing, rather than saving first and then spending later. The result for governments and households is that more and more income actually goes on repaying loans.

In most Western countries, the huge public debt is more or less matched by publicly held assets (schools, hospitals, etc.) so the net position is zero. The real wealth of nations (perhaps 5–6 times the annual national income) is held privately by the top decile of society and concentrated mostly in the top centile who can then lend money to governments to service their huge public debts. There are three main methods of reducing these public debts – taxes on capital, inflation or austerity (reduced public spending towards a balanced budget) (Piketty, 2014).

Leap-frogging old mistakes

And yet many poor countries need a growing financial sector as they develop, and many poor people around the world will need greater access to financial facilities. The rapid and recent expansion of M-Pesa (a mobile banking service facilitated by smartphones or even not-so-smart-phones) in Kenya is clear evidence of this need. But in the West, the banks are very big. Some are too big to fail, too big to sail, and too big to jail. Their failure would prevent people from paying bills and receiving wages. High personal remuneration in the banking sector does not reflect high productivity. Financial capital is attracted by the impression that there are high profits to be made, but King thinks this is often overstated. For the banks, it is a case of heads we win, tails you (the taxpayer) lose! (King, 2016). So there are many lessons here that the developing world could learn from to avoid the pitfalls of the past. Skipping the banking crises, and leapfrogging the fossil fuel dependency into new energy technologies, will allow them to thrive for decades to come without degrading their environment.

Berry maintains that there is now a growing perception, and not just among a few experts, that we are entering a time of inescapable limits. We are not likely to be granted another world to plunder in compensation for our pillage of this one. The hope that we can cure the ills of industrialism with the homoeopathy of more technology seems at last to be losing status. We are, in short, coming under pressure to understand ourselves as limited creatures in a limited world, in contradiction to the likes of Steven Pinker who believe in boundless progress.

We are capable of living not only within natural limits but also within cultural limits, which are self-imposed. We may elect to respond with the self-restraints implied in the attributes of neighbourliness, stewardship, thrift, temperance, generosity, care, kindness, friendship, loyalty and love. Berry knows that the idea of such limitations will horrify some people, maybe most people, for we have long encouraged ourselves to feel at home on 'the cutting edges' of knowledge and power. But we confuse limits with confinement. The Appalachian Mountains and forests we have destroyed in the pursuit of coal are gone forever. It is now too late to use thriftily the first half of the world's supply of oil. In the art of living we can only start again with what remains. From now on we are going to find a limit beyond which there will be no more. To start slowing down, with the idea of avoiding catastrophe, is a rational choice and a viable one if we can recover the necessary political sanity. Of course, it makes sense to consider alternative energy sources and perhaps work on how to desalinate the oceans to combat drought. But also we will have to re-examine the economic structures of our life, and conform them to the tolerances and limits of our earthly places (Berry, 2017). Alldred feels that these individual limits are insufficient and that systemic change is needed much more than individual epiphanies. And those ten attributes listed above do not cover any of the systemic forces that also need to change in overcoming the depredations of capitalism in any sensible time frame (Alldred, personal communication, 2018). In short, we must proceed with a **revalued standard of living/lifestyle** that acknowledges all these different types of limits.

CHAPTER 5

SIMPLE ECONOMIC COMPLEXITY

Economics is about choices, it is about incentives – but is it a simple subject or a very complicated one? This needs to be examined in some detail. Are people really capable of expecting the unexpected? To understand and weather economic booms and slumps requires a special approach to thinking about uncertainty. We cling to the 'illusion of certainty' in monetary matters. Newspapers and television are only too willing to print the latest forecast of, say, national income with a degree of precision that defies belief and far exceeds the ability of statisticians to measure it. Many thought it was Mervyn King's job, as Governor of the Bank of England, to have an official crystal ball in order to tell them what the future held. He would refer them to Voltaire – 'Doubt is not a pleasant condition, but certainty is an absurd one'. King outlines two types of uncertainty: **Risk** concerns events where it is possible to define the nature of the future outcome; **Radical uncertainty** concerns events where it is not possible to define, or even imagine, all the possible future outcomes.

Prices

In the secular world, King contends that coping strategies are especially important in financial markets because these markets are a link between the present and the future. But the very complexity of markets and derivatives can mislead the unwary into thinking that they are hedging risks while in fact they remain exposed to great uncertainty and potential losses (King, 2016). The various financial crashes over the years have taught us that money is not so certain, but we are still repeatedly tempted to put our trust in it. We are just as repeatedly warned in the Bible not to do so and of course the Bible's view of the future extends beyond old age into eternity (Beynon, 2011). The value and price of everything should be seen in this context.

Prices certainly do matter at one level. When Malawi, Uganda, Lesotho and Kenya stopped charging school fees, enrolments increased dramatically. German feed-in tariffs for households triggered transformative national investments in wind, solar, hydro and biomass energy technologies. But setting a price is like striking a match: it sparks intense interest but that spark ignites both power and danger – if it becomes all-consuming, it may transform the very ground across which it burns. Colombia's experiments with educational cash incentive schemes for school enrolment unexpectedly caused a large dropout rate among girls not selected for incentives. When market norms displace social norms, the effects can be hard to reverse. Instead of engaging existing intrinsic commitments, such as pride in cultural heritage, respect for the living world and trust in the community, some incentive schemes inadvertently serve to erode those very values and replace them with financial motivation. And price setting does not deal with all settings, for example the African rhinoceros does not increase its fertility as the value of rhino horn increases. So as Raworth (2017) warns,

> *Beware before you strike a match or start a market:*
> *you never know what riches it may reduce to ashes (Raworth, 2017).*

Markets can be liquid one day and illiquid the next, as happened on 19 October 1987, 'Black Monday'. The future is simply unknowable. So, in a capitalist economy, money, banking, and financial markets are institutions that have evolved to provide a way of coping with an unpredictable future (King, 2016). But Christians believe ultimately that the 'money-god' cannot deliver on its promises. It cannot secure health or happiness; it cannot ward off anxiety or fear; it cannot control the future; it cannot guarantee anything (Beynon, 2011). We need a better coping strategy; we need a **revalued standard of living**. Many in the First World will need to change the way they live – consume less, travel less, strive less, compete less and work less. There is contentment to be found in following such a path: being instead of doing.

King believes that central banks need a coping strategy too. Most central banks are youthful and their twin objectives are price stability (in good times) and the provision of liquidity as a 'lender of last resort' (in bad times).

Over the years, governments have been unable to resist the temptation to debase the currency – printing money to finance their expenditures and departing from the path of 'righteousness' in order to obtain short-term benefits, by stimulating the economy prior to an election in the hope that the inflationary cost will only become apparent to the electorate after the vote. In the past, when the costs (in terms of lost output and employment) of adhering to the gold standard appeared too high, governments simply suspended the convertibility of their currency into gold. More recently, the use of printing money led to the failure to control inflation, for example in the 1970s in the UK (King, 2016).

Complex worlds

Surely it is time, in Western democracy, to realise that those on the right of the political spectrum have some good ideas and that those on the left of the political spectrum also have some good ideas. Both sides have some dangerously bad ideas too. A wise government would select the best solutions to issues from whichever source and reject the rest of the political dogma, which ignores economic complexity. Raworth recognises the complexity in economics. So her **fourth suggestion** is to **get savvy with systems and move from mechanical equilibrium to dynamic complexity**. People used to live relatively short lives in small groups, learned from quick feedback and had little impact on their wider surroundings. But these brain traits leave us ill-equipped when the world turns out to be dynamic, unstable and unpredictable. The nineteenth century microeconomic inheritance is the supply and demand diagram/theory – an iconic pair of crossing lines: the point at which price matches supply with demand is the point of market equilibrium. But the theory is deeply flawed at the macroeconomic level – this was realised by some in the 1970s but ignored by others all the way up to the 2008 financial crash. US and European banks had bet heavily on US 'sub-prime' mortgages: home loans issued to those who did not qualify for normal mortgages; these often had low initial 'teaser' interest rates, which rose sharply after a set term. The loans were sold to investment banks, which bundled them into pools of mortgage-backed securities, then sliced these up into smaller pieces and sold them on to investors – promising good returns and low risks. While house prices rose, everyone profited: home buyers, bankers, and investors. But, starting in 2006, US house prices slumped nationwide. By September 2008, three per cent of US mortgage holders had defaulted. The bubble had burst, and the result was a devastating chain reaction, which ripped through the system. Insurers were sucked in via 'credit default swaps': $62 trillion in credit was insured in this way. A vast US federal bailout was announced. By the end of 2008, the Federal Reserve had pumped more than $1 trillion into the economy. In the UK, the rescue package totalled £500 billion in loans and guarantees. Governments across northern Europe took similar steps. Iceland's three biggest banks collapsed, bankrupting the nation (*The Week*, 2018).

Most economic researchers will come to believe that the economy is a complex system that belongs within complexity science. At the heart of systems thinking lie three deceptively simple concepts: stocks and flows, feedback loops (positive/reinforcing and negative/balancing) and delays. But their interaction is complex. Admittedly, more of this complexity relates to the First and Second Worlds than to the Third World. The demolition of the Berlin Wall in 1989, the 2008 collapse of Lehman Brothers and the imminent collapse of the Greenland ice sheet have much in common. They each have visible tipping points from accumulated pressure – be it the gradual build-up of political protest, the build-up of sub-prime mortgages or the build-up of greenhouse gases. Due to the scale and interconnectedness of the global economy, many economic effects that were treated as 'externalities' have turned into defining social and economic crises, and addressing these effects is of critical concern for creating an economy that enables us all to thrive (Raworth, 2017).

Confronted with radical uncertainty and complexity, it is natural that households and businesses make occasional 'mistakes', which can accumulate into substantial deviations, of spending and output, from a sustainable path. The cost of permitting the continuation of a large and growing disequilibrium is a crash at some point in the future, followed by economic stagnation (King, 2016). Marx is still relevant on some of the causes of crises in capitalism. Terry Eagleton, Professor of English Literature at Lancaster University, also stresses, in *Why Marx Was Right*, the modernity of Marx's thinking and how, for example, he saw the nature of social class shifting with the progress of capitalism: 'As long ago as the mid-nineteenth century, he is to be found writing of the "constantly growing number of the middle-classes" ... men and women "situated midway between the workers on the one side and the capitalists on the other"'. This is a long way from the hackneyed dichotomy of proletariat and bourgeoisie (Eagleton, 2011).

And we should neither take multinational corporations for the villains that they have often been portrayed as, nor for the munificent benefactors of developing countries. Limited liability has underpinned the growth of modern capitalism, but with globalisation the abuses of limited liability have become global in scale; without the reforms, they could become far worse. The lesson is simple: incentives matter, and the international community must work harder to ensure that the incentives facing corporations are better aligned with those they touch, especially the less powerful in the developing world (Stiglitz, 2006).

Counterintuitive though it sounds, when it comes to finance, stability breeds instability (Minsky, 1977). The confidence bubble will rise until prices eventually don't keep pace with expectations – crash time! Guess what happens post-crash? Confidence gradually rebuilds all over again in a rolling cycle of dynamic disequilibrium. Now, a better new disequilibrium model of the global economy that takes the feedbacks of banks, debt and money seriously is the Minsky systems-dynamics computer programme (Raworth, 2017).

Governments need to invest more time and energy into setting the right example of living within their means to avoid these boom/bust cycles. A balanced budget is vital. At one level economics is very simple: <u>income should equal expenditure</u>. This is the message that governments should be sending to their populations. Individuals would be well advised to avoid 'buy now, pay later'. Judging by the current heavy workload of debt advice agencies such as 'Christians Against Poverty' there is much to be done in this regard. Of course, a humane balanced budget in the Third World (such as Mauritania, Mali or Malawi) is impossible because of the constraints of geography, climate and disease (Sachs, 2005). Impossible, that is, unless something more radical is offered, such as a universal basic income financed by a progressive global wealth tax.

To reverse growing disequilibrium, many countries need to correct their balance of trade, placing an emphasis on exports abroad. This is more important than stimulating more consumer demand at home. Poor countries also need to be allowed to join in. Raworth reminds us that inequality features only as a peripheral concern in the world of equilibrium economics. But in the complex unequal world that we actually inhabit – where powerful reinforcing feedbacks are in play – virtuous cycles of wealth and vicious cycles of poverty can send otherwise similar people spiralling to the opposite ends of the income–distribution spectrum (the hourglass society). Between 1988 and 2008, the majority of countries worldwide saw rising inequality within their borders, resulting in a hollowing-out of their middle classes. Over those same twenty years, global inequality fell slightly overall (mostly thanks to falling poverty in China) but increased significantly at the extremes.

The great middle-class squeeze is not at an end. Education may not have much influence on what happens because many rich societies are already near the upper limit in terms of quantity of education, and many people are already overqualified for what they do. Success might depend on the chance of having been born well and having luck in life. It is hard to imagine that a system with such high inequality could be politically stable. Only in the middle of the twentieth century were rising incomes accompanied by decreasing inequality. It is not certain that increased taxation and social transfers, hyperinflation, nationalisation of property and wars will again drive down inequality in the future. Globalisation makes capital income very difficult to tax because it is so mobile. Hyperinflation has fallen out of favour as a means of reining in creditors and big proprietors. No more land will be nationalised. And no sensible person can wish for global wars again. If market income and capital wealth inequality could be controlled and curbed, government redistribution could be much less important, satisfying those who wish for a smaller state (Milanovic, 2016). Getting into the Doughnut requires reversing these widening gaps of income and wealth, and cannot be done simply by virtuous individuals vowing to live a more sustainable life. Again, we all need to move to a revalued standard of living and a new fairer global economic system.

To avoid overshooting the Doughnut requires understanding the dynamics of climate change. When it comes to tackling climate change, unlike in banking crises, there is no chance of a last-minute bailout. Many people have a surprisingly poor intuitive grasp of how stock-flow dynamics work. Just as a bathtub will only start to empty if the water pours in from the tap more slowly than it drains out of the plughole, so CO_2 concentration will only fall if new emissions flow in more slowly than CO_2 is drawn out. Policy makers currently think it is easier to stabilise greenhouse gases and stop warming than it actually is, and they really need to recognise the scale of energy transformation required to bring ourselves back within the planetary boundary for climate change. We will return to this subject in more detail in Chapter 8.

Global economic development trends echo the conditions under which earlier civilisations have collapsed. A society is far less adept at changing if it has a small elite, quite separate from the masses, making short-term decisions which diverge from the long-term interests of all – it is a blueprint for trouble. The business-as-usual scenario does not end well: already we have transgressed several planetary boundaries, millions of people still face extreme deprivation, and the richest ten per cent own half of the world's financial wealth (Raworth, 2017).

On the personal level, the economics of a household budget may be simplified to 'income equals expenditure'. However, on the global level, complex economic dynamics are at work. It is now time to intervene strategically in this complexity to address social injustice (inequality) and ecological damage (climate change) with some sensible redistribution and regeneration.

CHAPTER 6

REDISTRIBUTION AND REGENERATION

Sᴜᴄ INCE THE LATE EIGHTEENTH century, the average life expectancy across the world has risen from thirty to seventy-one years and, for the more fortunate individuals in some countries, up to eighty-one years.

> *When the Enlightenment began, a third of the children born in the richest parts of the world died before their fifth birthday; today that fate befalls only six per cent of the children in the poorest parts. Their mothers, too, were freed from tragedy: one per cent in the richest countries did not live to see their newborns, a rate triple that of the poorest countries today, which continues to fall. In those poor countries, lethal infectious diseases are in steady decline; some of them afflicting just a few dozen people, soon to follow smallpox into extinction (Pinker, 2018).*

Lessons in redistribution

But things could be even better. There are lessons from the past. In 1795, the magistrates of Speenhamland, England, gathered to radically reform assistance for the poor. They started by supplementing incomes up to subsistence level for **all** the needy in the district. The larger the family, the greater were the payments. This was different from the Elizabethan Poor Laws, which separated the deserving poor (into almshouses) from those who had to be forced to work (sold off to landowners). Gradually in Speenhamland, hunger and hardship decreased. Yet, the 1832 Royal Commission survey into Speenhamland blamed the basic income for a population explosion, wage reductions, and increased immoral conduct. But historians have since discovered that much of the Commission's text had been written **before** the data were collected; only ten per cent of questionnaires were returned, and most of those were not actual beneficiaries! So a new, draconian Poor Law ensued, workhouses and all. And 150 years later this bogus science managed to derail President Nixon's Basic Income Bill. Things could have been different had Nixon's plan gone ahead; the ramifications would have been huge. No longer would there be such a thing as the 'deserving' or 'undeserving' poor. Had the United States gone down the basic income route, there is little doubt other countries would have followed suit. Now, will we ever be able to shake off the dogma that if you want money, you have to work for it?

'Our modern welfare states have come to look increasingly like surveillance states. Yet economists have denounced the "unemployment industry" (job-application workshops, LinkedIn training) all along. The costs are huge and performing mindless tasks leaves less time for parenting, education, and looking for a real job. Every application for assistance has its own debasing, money-guzzling red tape protocol. This isn't a war on poverty; it's a war on the poor. It all boils down to a pointless distinction between "two types of poor" – the fallacy that a life without poverty is a privilege you have to work for, rather than a right we all deserve.'

Bregman feels it is time to look again at a universal basic income (Bregman, 2018).

The great enemies for neoliberal economists are not just Keynesianists in the US, but also the social democrats in Europe and the 'developmentalists' in the Global South. After the coup in Chile, the US sought to totally remake economic policy as an experiment in line with free market principles. The results were a disaster. There was some recovery after 1978, buoyed by speculative finance from abroad, but in 1982 the economy in Chile crashed hard. Eventually Pinochet had to renationalise many of the privatised companies and banks. The only people who benefited from the new economic regime were the elite – Chile became one of the most unequal societies in the world. The experiment could not have been implemented in a democratic government.

The crisis of 'stagflation' (inflation and recession) in the 1970s may have been a consequence of specific historic events, but it was blamed on Keynesianism. In rolled tight monetarist policy (i.e. targeting low inflation), 'supply-side economics' and the banking deregulations of Ronald Reagan and Margaret Thatcher. These policies drove social inequality to unprecedented levels in the US and UK. Productivity increased steadily while wages stagnated, effectively shifting an increasing proportion of profits from workers to the owners of capital (Hickel, 2017).

Old and new greens

Next, it is instructive to listen to Paul Kingsnorth as he reminds us of the problems evolving inside the green movement over recent years. The year in which the 'Limits to Growth' report was published, 1972, perhaps marked the start of the green movement. The green future looked bright at the 1992 Earth Summit in Rio de Janeiro. However, rather than push for the recalibration of the international trade rules to conform with the requirements of climate protection, the Rio Earth Summit has ensured that liberalised trade and an expanding global economy have been protected against trade-restrictive climate policies (Klein, 2014). But more than two decades on, things look rather different. Every environmental problem identified at the original summit has gotten worse and there is no sign of this changing.

The 'old environmentalists' ('old greens') have struggled to change population behaviours. They focused on promoting limits to consumption rates and carbon emissions. Although their dire predictions have been broadly correct, the impact of their message has been very limited. So instead, the neo-environmentalists view nature as tough and still able to adapt to human development. They contend that pre-industrial culture has been idealised and has no lessons for the future. Their beliefs in markets, the scientific method and new technologies mean that they are less concerned by limits and contend that the wild is dead and the rest of nature is for people to use. But the fact remains that a world of nine billion 'middle class' consumers is not a sustainable future. Raworth feels:

> *Today's economy is divisive and degenerative by default.*
> *Tomorrow's economy must be distributive and regenerative by design. (Raworth, 2017)*

An economy that is distributive by design is one whose dynamics tend to disperse and circulate value as it is created. Such effective systems tend to have three properties – mutually supportive networks, self-organisation and resilience. Mutually supportive networks will ensure that the financial sector is in service to the productive economy, which in turn is in service to life. Mutually supportive networks are better than healthy hierarchies, no matter how 'healthy'. Much self-organising goes on in the marketplace, in the commons, in local communities and in the household. The state should support all in doing so. Building diversity and redundancy into economic structures enhances the economy's resilience, making it far more effective in adapting to future shocks and pressures (Raworth, 2017).

So Raworth's **fifth idea** is that **local and global economies need to be transformed to make them distributive and regenerative by design**. The motto of 'no pain, no gain', as far as the economy is concerned, is a false belief based not on evidence but on that erroneous yet deeply influential diagram – the Kuznets curve. Rising inequality is a deeply damaging policy choice with multiple repercussions that push humanity further out of the Doughnut. Rather, modern economics should regard inequality as a failure of economic design and should, instead of focusing primarily on redistributing income earned, focus on aiming to redistribute wealth too (Raworth, 2017).

Postcode redistribution

Sider has looked for Biblical models of economic justice – capital in an agricultural society, the Year of Jubilee, the Sabbatical Year, tithing and gleaning, Jesus' new community, the early church Jerusalem model and economic *koinonia* (community) (Sider, 2015). Of course, Chilton countered that the Hebrew law of the Jubilee was not a Poor Law. Its primary intent and function had nothing to do with the alleviation of poverty as such. Certainly, it did affect the status of certain poor people. But that was only incidental to its true purpose. In fact – in contrast to the laws on tithing, the laws on gleaning, lending, and slavery – most of the poor may not have been affected by the observance of the Jubilee at all. Rather he believed that price and capital controls and expropriation of lands and businesses all require guns and men who are prepared to use them. Apart from when under the threat of violence or coercive enforcement of the regulations, no landowner or businessman will relinquish his property (Chilton, 1981). A more enlightened view would be, rather than extolling the pre-eminence of private property, the sharing of all God-given resources (Blomberg, 1999). No matter what particular fuels or minerals are under your feet, everyone is under the postcode EA...RTH!

In the more recent past, redistribution fell into three broad categories: progressive income taxes and transfers; labour market protections such as a minimum wage; and providing public services (health, education and social housing). Now economists in high-income countries advocate raising top marginal income tax rates along with higher taxes on interest, rent and dividends. Social activists have applied pressure to pay living wages. But these do not get to the root of economic inequalities, because they focus on redistributing **income**, not the **wealth** that generates it. Tackling inequality at its root calls for democratising the ownership of wealth. Five opportunities stand out, concerning who controls land, money creation, enterprise, technology and knowledge.

Transparent tax

Before looking at each of these in detail, what about tax as a method of redistribution? By the autumn of 2010 in the UK, the big economic question was how the two-year-old financial crisis was going to be paid for. While unprecedented public spending cuts were being lined up, the billions lost to tax avoidance remained some way down the political agenda. In his book, *The Great Tax Robbery*, Richard Brooks asserts that the HM Revenue and Customs (HMRC) – big business relationship needed jettisoning: 'no cosy conferences, no favours, no deals and understandings; no inside tracks and no private access'. It had become a covert subsidy to big business in Britain. Politicians needed to take on not just tax dodging but other scourges, such as excessive boardroom pay. If 'austerity' programmes were to carry public support, they needed to look like they were confronting greed at the top too (Brooks, 2010).

'Dave Hartnett, the former boss of HM Revenue & Customs, has taken a job with HSBC Bank since leaving HMRC, holding a place on a committee set up to advise the bank on the best possible standards in the wake of its recent travails. In addition to revelations about the activities of its Swiss unit in helping clients to duck tax, the bank was hit with a £1.2bn penalty by the US authorities after it emerged that its Mexican operation had been used by drug gangs to launder dirty cash. They had also accused HSBC of being involved in sanctions busting.'

'Mr Hartnett defended the role, saying he was attracted to it because it would involve him in being part of efforts to clean up the bank. He said he believed in the programme set out by the bank's under-fire chief executive Stuart Gulliver, and he followed all the requisite procedures required for civil servants taking jobs with private industry before signing on the dotted line.

He also defended the deals entered into between HMRC and the authorities in Lichtenstein and Switzerland, which have enabled people not already under investigation to declare their holdings and pay tax without being prosecuted. 'It still sounds like gamekeeper turned poacher! MPs contrasted the treatment of those running small businesses or found to have been overpaid tax credits by HMRC with wealthy individuals using overseas bank accounts to evade or avoid tax' (Moore, 2015).

When it comes to taxation, the need for fairness is especially acute: if the privileged are not paying their fair share, compliance with tax laws can fall dramatically, with economically ruinous consequences. With some straightforward offshore planning, the biggest multinationals can take their tax rates way below any headline rate the government announces. They do not need loopholes, they just follow the very laws they themselves helped draft. Still too much tax law remains at the service of tax avoidance. Potential tax avoiders need to be given strong reasons **not** to indulge in tax dodging, to counter the obvious motivations to do so. The best deterrent is far greater openness. Multinational corporations must publish what tax they pay in each country and territory in which they have any presence. With no sign that opportunities to divert profits into tax havens will end (quite the reverse), the price of tax avoidance is loss of reputation (Brooks, 2013). How high this reputational price actually is within the financial industry when 'they are all at it on behalf of shareholders' is open to question.

The Washington-based organisation Global Financial Integrity (GFI) calculates that up to sixty-five per cent of total global illicit outflows have to do with corrupt commercial tax evasion. Each year $1.1 trillion flows illegally out of developing countries and into foreign banks and tax havens via hot money and trade mis-invoicing. The problem with tax havens is that they induce 'tax competition', making it difficult for governments to make rational decisions about tax legislation. Given the roles various European countries have in maintaining the tax haven system, it seems strange that rich countries appear in 'corruption-free yellow' on the Transparency International map. Public perceptions of corruption do not reflect reality, which should include illicit outflows, anonymous companies, secrecy jurisdictions and tax havens (Hickel, 2017).

Disclosure of tax payments would ideally form a worldwide corporate financial reporting standard. Tax payments could become as routine a part of a company's financial announcements as its sales and profit figures. These should be placed on the public record, whether executed by individuals or corporations. If there is nothing wrong with the business, what is there to hide? If non-domiciled or non-resident reliefs are claimed, they should be totally transparent.

The laws themselves need to be made fairer. When it comes to corporate taxation, action is required at both the international and domestic levels to end the now standard practice for multinationals to shunt their income into the world's tax havens. The rules of this game, largely imposed by the Organisation for Economic Cooperation and Development (controlled by the world's wealthier nations), should be amended to allow governments to tax profits based on companies' real physical presence and override internal reorganisations effected for tax purposes, moving capital and assets into special tax haven subsidiary companies. The European Union now embraces some tax havens whose club membership makes them as equally toxic as the traditional tropical island variety. What is required for change is the political will (Brooks, 2013).

Piketty asks, 'Are the rich countries really poor?' To judge by official statistics (IMF), it would seem that the net asset position of most wealthy countries (excluding Germany and Japan) vis-à-vis the rest of the world is negative, equivalent to about –4% of global GDP in 2010. Of course, this should be counterbalanced by poor countries owning more assets in the rich countries, but this is not the case! Is the earth then owned by Mars? No, the answer was provided by Gabriel Zucman in 2015, exploiting previously unused Swiss bank data which showed that large amounts of unreported financial assets are held in tax havens – perhaps ten per cent of global GDP! (Zucman, 2015).

When it comes to the secret tax havens hiding the world's untaxed trillions, a new standard for forcing them to provide information to the world's tax authorities is urgently needed. The EU Savings Tax Directive and the much more robust US Foreign Account Tax Compliance Act (FATCA) should be supported, reinforced and exported. Domestic law should close down tax havens within its direct sphere of influence. Tax law should make it far harder to get money into other recalcitrant tax havens in the first place. For example, Britain should tear up the tax agreement with Switzerland that enshrines tax haven secrecy and decriminalises offshore tax fraud (Brooks, 2013), and tackle the myriad of other tax havens supported by the UK (the Isle of Man, the Channel Islands, Gibraltar, the various Caribbean territories, etc.).

Governments often tax what they easily can rather than what they really should. The emphasis should be on taxing wealth rather than employment income. A global wealth tax on capital wealth, investments, shares and dividends held in any jurisdiction worldwide is sensible. A progressive global tax on capital is the most appropriate response to the inequality r > g as well as to the inequality of returns to capital as a function of the initial stake. This idea needs some renewed attention – taxing all capital (land, property, shares, dividends, inheritance, etc.) explicitly for the globalised patrimonial capitalism of the twenty-first century. Sovereign wealth funds could then be set up to benefit whole populations. It will only really work in conjunction with a new **all-encompassing financial transparency worldwide.** In 2015, in his book *The Hidden Wealth of Nations*, Zucman used the systematic anomalies in international investment positions to show that the net foreign asset positions of rich countries are generally underestimated because they don't capture most of the assets held by households in offshore tax havens. Based on his calculations, he finds about eight per cent of the global financial wealth of households, or $7.6 trillion, to be held in tax havens, three quarters of which goes undeclared. Research published by Zucman, Tørsløv and Weir, in June 2018, showed that Ireland is the largest <u>corporate tax haven</u> in the world, even larger than the entire Caribbean corporate tax haven system. Much of Zucman's other research deals with the effects of the <u>G20</u>'s attempted crackdown on tax havens and corporate tax havens, cross-border taxation and multinational profit shifting, the long-term relationship between wealth and inheritance, and the trajectory of wealth inequality in the United States. But **modern corporate tax havens** (such as Ireland, the Netherlands, and Singapore) differ from **traditional corporate tax havens** (such as Bermuda, the Cayman Islands, and Jersey) in their ability to maintain OECD-compliance (see Appendix 3). Ireland and Luxembourg are in the top fifteen per cent of the <u>GDP-per-capita tax haven proxy</u> list. The distortion can lead to over-leverage in the haven's economy (and property bubbles), making them prone to severe credit cycles. Tax havens should become obsolete.

Andy Beckett, in *The Guardian*, 7th September 2018, reviewing Oliver Bullough's book *Moneyland*, picks out that money flows across frontiers, but laws do not! Until this situation changes, the lawyers, bankers and drafters of deliberately loose financial laws will continue to prosper. Meanwhile, governments will continue to be starved of revenue, global inequality will grow, economies will be destabilised and struggling voters will blame everyone – poor immigrants, liberal elites – except those actually responsible for creating the destructive offshore world (Bullough in Beckett, 2018).

High taxation for the use of environmental resources like water and oil, and for the creation of environmental pollutants including plastic, should also be the norm everywhere. Water rates, for instance, should be universally progressive. Aviation travel, for business or pleasure, should be discouraged with targeted carbon taxes, especially in the age of 'FaceTime' and 'Skype'.

Taxation of retired populations should be much more progressive in the Western world. For example, all over-65-year-olds earning over £65,000 should pay a sixty-five per cent tax rate on these excess earnings or deferred income. Younger wealth creators should be subject to less **income** tax to encourage inward investment in regenerative enterprises, which benefit the planet long-term. Laws need to be changed to enable governments to do 'cash grabs' from excessive occupational pensions that are unjust to future generations. The wealth locked up in property should be extracted and put to good use through mansion taxes and suitable taxes on rental income. Fairness in education for future generations requires a retrospective university education tax, backdated to the post-war era. There are lots of ideas, all aimed at more equality and especially at bringing the top ten per cent earners and super-rich back towards the mean. Everyone should be racing to the middle.

These ideas were anathema to David Chilton. He felt the notion that there can be any such thing as 'unfair profit' is one of the oldest socialist ideas, produced by two problems which are central to the very nature of socialism: envy and ignorance. He contended that envy is the greatest disease of our age, often confused with jealousy and covetousness, which have to do with wanting the possessions and privileges of others. He felt that envy is much more insidious and deadly because envy is the feeling that *someone else's having something is to blame for the fact that you do not have it'* (Chilton, 1981). Not many people whose thinking is faith-based or secular, looking at current global inequality, would agree with Chilton. Ron Sider acknowledges that a market economy is an economic arrangement in which the bulk of the wealth and means of production are privately owned and most wages and prices are set by supply and demand. But he points out that a pure laissez-faire economy (where the government never intervenes in economic life) does not exist (Sider, 2015). Tax revenue is important and influential.

So what should governments do with all this new tax revenue? Firstly, on a supranational basis, set up a global universal basic income fund for all peoples, and secondly the First World governments should pay off national debts and cancel Third World debts. Introduced properly this might lessen the need for the myriad of more complicated taxes mentioned above. Next, an honest and 'level playing field' conversation with the Third World can take place to remove tariffs and expand overseas development aid to allow poor countries to 'catch up' in the most environmentally-friendly and regenerative way possible. Although care needs to be taken with the definition of 'catch up', because: (a) 'here' is not where people in poorer countries necessarily need to get to; (b) it presupposes a development agenda that would be mainly set by the West (Global North) who would be offering the wherewithal for poor countries to fund their progress; and (c) it presupposes 'we' stay here comfortably, whereas we need to fundamentally rethink our position in this world of global inequality and make some significant sacrifices to foster real justice. A sensible path to follow would be Raworth's five key areas of opportunity for **redistribution**:

1. Who owns the land?
For people whose livelihoods and culture depend upon the land, secure land rights are essential. What determines house value? Location, location, location. Some land-value taxes are in use, for example, in Denmark, Kenya

and Australia. The problem is that there really isn't a housing market in places like Chad or Namibia. Approaches to distributive land design must fit the people and the place, and may well work best when they combine the market, the commons and the state. During the food-price crisis of 2007, investors seized the opportunity to buy up millions of acres of land around the world for agricultural production of both food and biofuels. Many of these purchases were land grabs converting smallholder production to commercial activity, thereby causing environmental damage and human harm. The land grabbers are always rich and the people displaced always poor. Land grabbing has been defended in the name of climate change amelioration, such as REDD (Reducing Emissions from Deforestation and forest Degradation). But it often leads to zero reduction in carbon emissions, as the whole idea behind carbon credits is to allow polluters to avoid reducing their emissions by buying their way around the rules (Hickel, 2017).

2. Who makes your money?

Money is, in essence, a social relationship based on trust. Commercial banks create money every time they offer loans or credit. Currently many investments do not redistribute wealth but simply push up the price of existing assets. If every bank loan were backed by someone else's savings it would prevent the build-up of debt-fuelled credit bubbles that can burst. State-owned banks could use money from the central bank to channel substantial zero-interest loans into investments for carbon-neutral housing and public transport ('Green Quantitative Easing QE'). After 2008, the price of commodities (for example, grain, metals, land and property) eventually rose but new investments in productive businesses didn't. Instead central banks could issue new money directly to every household to pay down debts ('People's QE'), a mechanism for Bregman's universal basic income. These radical ideas would promote greater equality, tending to favour the low-income and indebted households rather than the asset rich.

In the commons, diverse communities can create their own complementary currencies to boost the local economy or reward work that is traditionally unpaid, although this will work better in leafy Surrey than in the Central African Republic. The way that money is designed has far reaching distributional implications.

3. Who owns your labour?

Stagnant wages have become a familiar story. Across all high-income countries, while workers' productivity grew by over five per cent from

2009 to 2014, their wages rose just 0.4%. Employees are cast as outsiders: a production cost, hired and fired as necessary. Shareholders who are never on the company premises are the ultimate insiders: their profits take priority. Rooted membership and stakeholder finance offer a better model and such enterprises are growing. It is about broadening economic power from the few to the many and changing from social indifference to social benefit. In the meantime, open borders would be transformative – lifting all migration barriers to allow anyone who wants to come into any economy and benefit from the advantages. Again, I will say more on this in Chapter 7.

4. Who owns the robots?

The digital revolution is far more significant than the invention of writing or printing (Engelbert, 2017). Now everyone can potentially become a 'prosumer' – both a maker and user in the peer-to-peer economy. But a parallel process of winner-takes-all dynamics is also in play. The Internet's strong network effects have transformed individual providers (for example, Google, Apple, Facebook) into digital monopolies running the global social commons, while arming themselves with patents to guard their privilege.

The digital revolution is also displacing people with near zero-humans-required production. Robots put millions of skilled and unskilled jobs at risk. Job creation in other fields simply cannot keep up – perhaps a few high-skill jobs, many low-skill jobs and nothing in between.

It is time to switch from taxing labour to taxing the use of non-renewable resources and to skilling people up in creativity, empathy, insight and human-contact jobs. Some advocate a 'robot dividend' for every citizen. But many nation states currently earn surprisingly little direct revenue from the multibillion-dollar digital economy despite having invested substantial public money into the research, development and infrastructure underpinning it. Royalties could be collected from co-owned public–private patents to distribute wealth widely – the social licensing concept.

5. Who owns the ideas?

The international regime of intellectual property rights has significantly shaped the control and distribution of knowledge for hundreds of years. But now patents and trademarks are stifling innovation. Free open-source software and hardware can solve this problem and radically decentralise the ownership of wealth in the commons, with a little state support, for example:

    a) Invest in ingenuity by teaching social entrepreneurship and problem solving in schools and universities

b) Ensure all publicly funded research becomes public knowledge

c) Prevent spurious patent and copyright applications from encroaching on the knowledge commons

d) Publicly fund community maker-spaces

e) Encourage the spread of civic organisations (Raworth, 2017).

Shorter working week

To this Bregman would add that it is time also to look at a shorter working week. In fact, even John Maynard Keynes felt that the greatest challenge for the twenty-first century would be leisure. He predicted that by 2030 we would be working just fifteen hours per week. John Stuart Mill proposed his own 'gospel of leisure'. The industrial revolution had brought the exact opposite of leisure – long hours, no vacations, and no weekends. In 1855, the stonemasons of Melbourne, Australia, were the first to secure an eight-hour workday. Henry Ford and the Ford Motor Company implemented a five-day workweek and increased productivity. A shorter workweek did not ruin the economy. But after World War II, leisure time continued its steady rise. Isaac Asimov, a futurologist, was only worried by one thing: the spread of boredom. Many of the predictions about the year 2062 have already come true – housekeeping robots, tanning beds, touchscreens, video chat – but so far the shorter workweek is not one of them because, in the 1980s, workweek reductions came to a grinding halt. Families became ever more pressed for time. No one saw the rapid changes in women's work patterns coming or that women's contribution to the family income would rise from two per cent to forty per cent. Thanks to modern technology, professionals now spend eighty to ninety hours per week either working or 'monitoring work and remaining accessible'.

Time is money. Economic growth can yield either more **leisure time** or more **consumption**. Since 1980, mostly consumption has increased, even as inequality has exploded, and this has been achieved on the credit card! And at the same time, the main argument against the shorter workweek is that we can't afford it!

In the UK, during the 'Winter of Discontent', Prime Minister Edward Heath decided on radical action and on January 1, 1974 imposed a three-day workweek. After things returned to normal, officials calculated that the extent of the loss of production was a grand total of only six per cent! Bregman feels a shorter working week would help with stress, climate change, accidents, unemployment, emancipation of women, ageing population issues, and inequality.

'There is simply not enough paid work to go around. And actually, this is good news. Yet, there is hardly a politician around still willing to endorse a shorter workweek, even with stress and unemployment in some countries surging to record levels' (Bregman, 2018).

In 1968, a garbage collectors' strike crippled New York in double-quick time but when the bankers of Ireland went on strike in 1970, the Irish economy sailed along as usual for a whole six months. How is it possible that all those agents of prosperity – the teachers, the police officers, and the nurses – are paid so poorly, while the so-called important, superfluous and even destructive bankers do so well? In a market economy things can work the wrong way round. As farms and factories grew more efficient, they accounted for a shrinking share of the economy. And the more productive agriculture and manufacturing became, the fewer people they employed. At the same time this shift generated more work in the service sector. Of course, proper credentials are needed to get a job as a consultant, accountant, programmer, advisor, broker or lawyer and generate immense wealth. We now have a system in which an increasing number of people can earn money without contributing anything tangible to society. The converse of this would be real social return on investment. The New Economics Foundation (NEF) has done some great work on SROI – Social Return on Investment. Although the value we create goes far beyond what can be captured in financial terms, this is, for the most part, the only type of value that is measured and accounted for. As a result, things that can be bought and sold take on a greater significance and many important things get left out. Decisions made like this may not be as good as they could be as they are based on incomplete information about full impacts. An up-to-date example would be the various projects on social prescribing taking place within the National Health Service, most of which have not been fully evaluated yet, but stakeholder feedback reports much value, particularly for the lonely, frail elderly, which cannot be measured completely in financial terms. (New Economics Foundation, 2009).

Regeneration

However, making money without creating anything of value is anything but easy. It takes talent, ambition and brains. But the fact that something is difficult does not automatically make it valuable. Complex financial products are, essentially, like a tax on the rest of the population. The financial sector redistributes wealth to the lucky few without generating value and without a democratic mandate. Beware the government, which cuts back on useful jobs in sectors like healthcare, education, and infrastructure while investing millions in the unemployment industry of training and surveillance. And beware the modern marketplace, which is not interested in usefulness, quality and innovation, but only profit. It has become increasingly profitable not to innovate. Too many bright minds now spend time dreaming up hyper-complex financial products. Imagine if all this talent were to be invested not in shifting wealth around, but in creating it. We can take a step towards a different world, again starting with taxes. A transactions tax is needed to rein in the financial industry and end high frequency trading which adds nothing of social value. We need to reverse the mass career switch from teachers and engineers to bankers and accountants. Higher taxes for top earners would serve, in economic science-speak, 'to reallocate talented individuals from professions that cause negative externalities to those that cause positive externalities'. (Bregman, 2017).

If you were to draw up a list of the most influential professions, teachers would rank among the highest, because teaching shapes the course of human history. Unfortunately the focus in education at present is on competencies, not values; on didactics, not ideals; on 'problem-solving ability', not which problems need solving. No doubt a skilful accountant untroubled by a conscience will find gainful employment in the future enabling multinationals to dodge taxes in the havens of Luxembourg and Switzerland. Instead, we should be posing a different question altogether: which knowledge and skills do we want our children to have in the future? Do we want more solidarity across race, gender and socioeconomic groups? Start in the social studies class. We need to free ourselves of the dogma that all work is meaningful and the fallacy that a higher salary is automatically a reflection of societal value. In fact, work that involves regeneration should perhaps be the most highly valued. For instance work in the **agricultural sphere**: food sovereignty – sharing fairly the costs of food systems; agroecology – working with nature in genetic and cultural diversity using sustainable methods based on a combination of modern science and local knowledge; animal welfare – maximising physical and psychological well-being; and sustainable diets. And work in the **environmental sphere**: environmental justice – substitution products as animal food substrates; nature conservation – maximising diversity in species and ecosystems; health and well-being; and sustainable lifestyles.

The inhabitants of the Land of Plenty have every reason to fear for their jobs with the breakneck development of driving robots, reading robots, talking, writing and calculating robots. They have become one of the strongest arguments in favour of a shorter workweek and a universal basic income. Welcome to the race against the machine.

The chip and the box – The number of transistors per microchip has been doubling every year. Also, shipping containers have become the standard unit of transport, greatly reducing the time ships spend in port, loading and unloading. Technology and globalisation are advancing hand in hand and faster than ever.

Labour versus capital – Technological progress has also meant that less wealth went to labour wages and more into the pockets of the owners of capital (r > g). For example, the emergence of online sellers led to the loss of millions of jobs in retail. The smaller the world gets, the fewer the number of winners. In the age of the chip, the box, and Internet retail, being just fractionally better than the rest means you've not only won the battle, you've won the war. The reality is that it takes fewer and fewer people to create a successful business, meaning that when a business succeeds, fewer and fewer people benefit and inequality increases.

Now, as we step out into a new century, the robots have suddenly picked up the pace. The great decoupling is the paradox of our era – 'Global productivity is at record levels, innovation has never been faster, and yet at the same time, we have a falling median income and we have fewer jobs'. Workforce (labour) productivity is defined by output volume divided by labour input. (Bregman, 2017).

Real median family income has not risen by the same extent, as shown overleaf. (Bureau of Labour Statistics, 2012).

> 'Today new jobs are mostly at the bottom of the pyramid – at supermarkets, fast-food chains and nursing homes. Labour market polarisation is the widening gap between 'lousy jobs' and 'lovely jobs' (Bregman, 2018).

Productivity, currently, may be static or slightly falling in the UK, but like our addiction to GDP, the emphasis on productivity is misplaced because the future is a shorter working week. Slowly but surely, in modern democracies, the middle class is crumbling. Asian, African or robot labour will always come cheaper. Eventually, even the sweatshops in Vietnam and Bangladesh will be automated too.

Remedies – Not much can be done to stop this trend, according to many economists. Anyone who hasn't managed to learn a skill that machines cannot

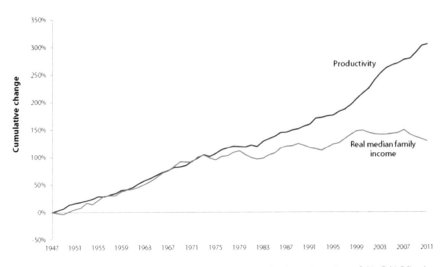

Source: Authors' analysis of Current Population Survey Annual Social and Economic Supplement *Historical Income Tables* (Table F-5) and Bureau of Labor Statistics, *Productivity - Major Sector Productivity and Costs Database (2012)*

master will be sidelined. So the Second Machine Age calls for more drastic measures than a revolution in education and welfare as before, but rather more radical measures like a shorter workweek and universal basic income.

The future of capitalism – In the end, it is we humans who decide how we want to shape our destiny. The richer we as a society become, the less effective the labour market will be at distributing prosperity. Different redistributions are needed – redistribution of money (basic income), redistribution of time (a shorter workweek), redistribution of taxation (on capital instead of labour income) and, of course, a redistribution of the robot dividend. (Bregman, 2018).

In summary, going global raises tough issues. A global tax on extreme personal wealth could raise additional funds, as would a global corporate tax, which closes tax loopholes and tax havens. But equally important would be the creation of Commons Trusts on a global scale. A commons trust is a legal entity responsible for protecting a shared asset that is inherited from past generations, or is presently being created, on behalf of current and future generations. Because it is common property – held in trust and not owned by anyone – the commons are insulated from any claims by private individuals, businesses, governments or other trusts. Each trust would cap overall ecological use, charge its users, whether for extracting water or offloading gases, and try to ensure that historic ecological debts are repaid. In money terms – how can you pay back citizens of the Amazon rainforest? Well, a globally funded universal basic income would be a start, encouraging equality of opportunity!

Instead of focusing on redistributing income alone, economists should also seek to redistribute wealth – be it the power to control land, money creation, enterprise, technology, knowledge or time – and should then harness the market, the commons and the state to drive a revolution in redistribution (Raworth, 2017). This needs to be a worldwide phenomenon; all nations need to take this message on board. This is best done by adopting policies which are locally adapted to the degree of development that a country has already undergone, and in a way that is regenerative in terms of planetary ecosystems. It is vitally important that individual nations are not inhibited from making these redistribution and regenerative changes for fear of falling behind in some competitive international race for resources. The United Nations could facilitate a new international deliberative democracy of debate and discussion, with the aim of reaching agreement or consensus upon which decisions can then be based to promote both redistribution and regeneration. However, the whole process of different 'tribes' making good decisions is fraught with difficulties. At present, the whole post-World War II architecture of international cooperation – the UN system – is dysfunctional and not fit for purpose. This is where we need to turn next.

CHAPTER 7

DECISION MAKING

IF WE ACCEPT DEMOCRACY as the least bad option for government, we must also accept that it faces big challenges – dishonesty, inequality, corruption and now technology. Pinker reminds us that humanity has tried to steer a course between the violence of anarchy (chaos) and the violence of tyranny.

> *Chaos is worse than tyranny. Early governments pacified the people they ruled, reducing internecine violence, but imposed a reign of terror that included slavery, harems, human sacrifice, summary executions and the torture and mutilation of dissidents and deviants. The alternative to a despot was even worse. The list of different types of governmental arrangements was outlined earlier. One can think of democracy as a form of government that threads the needle, exerting just enough force to prevent people from preying on each other without the government preying on the people themselves. Therefore democracy is a major contributor to human flourishing. Democracies have higher rates of economic growth, fewer wars and genocides, healthier and better-educated citizens and virtually no famines. The world has become more democratic, though not in a steadily rising tide (Pinker, 2018).*

Dishonesty

There are important decisions regarding redistribution to be taken politically in all countries. Western democracies, in particular, need to be honest with themselves, and the important institutions of state, including central banks, need to be honest and transparent with their populations. Any requirement for transparency in a central bank's deliberations should have the aim of improving the quality of its decisions. Central banks are powerful and have the ability to redistribute money quickly in times of crisis. It is also important for central banks to be honest about what they know and what they do not know. Pre-2008, financiers claimed to have found a way to banish risk, when in fact they had simply lost track of it. And in conjunction with deregulation in the late 1990s, risk-taking was encouraged (King, 2016).

Governments also need to be honest. It was extremely disconcerting recently in the UK to see a sensible policy change, regarding National Insurance contributions by the self-employed and attempts to get to grips with the looming crisis in financing social care provision, so quickly reversed by poorly informed public pressure. A modest increase in NI contributions for the self-employed was a step towards greater fairness and an equitable long-term policy but it became victim to nervous elected representatives worried about their personal prospects at the next hustings.

Another example of dishonesty by decision makers was the so-called 'dementia tax' fiasco prior to the 2017 General Election in the UK. The Tory manifesto unveiled a surprising pledge to shake up the way care for the elderly is funded. Currently those in residential care have to pay for it themselves if they have assets above £23,250. People can defer payment until after they die, meaning they do not have to sell their house while they are still alive or while a surviving partner lives in it. It was announced during the election campaign that this rule would also apply to so-called domiciliary care – care at home – if the Tories won. It meant those receiving home care would have to pay towards it and the value of their home would be included in their assets, which could be clawed back by councils. The Conservatives started by being brutally honest and said they were equalising an unfair system – and also quadrupling the savings or assets anyone can protect to £100,000. The Demos think tank said 'hundreds of thousands of the poorest older people' would benefit from raising the threshold. The shake-up was to be funded by ending the winter fuel allowance for well-off pensioners. Those who receive state-funded care at home would have been worse off if they had assets of more than £100,000 (certainly not a trivial amount!) – such as if they own their home – under the proposals. But immediately traditional Tory supporters said it was an attack on middle-class OAPs who want their children to inherit their property. Others accused the Conservatives of 'forcing those who need social care to pay for it with their homes' and Liberal Democrat Leader, Tim Farron, said it was a 'callous blow for people who have dementia and other long-term conditions, like multiple sclerosis and motor neurone disease, and of course their families – it is not just a massive mistake but a cruel attack on vulnerable people the length and breadth of this country'.

Health Secretary Jeremy Hunt declared that it was dishonest to ignore that social care costs get borne by taxpayers and 'we don't think that's fair on different generations'; he defended the plans, saying everyone would know they could pass on at least £100,000 to their children. He said: 'You could have a situation where someone who owns a house worth £1 million or £2 million, and has expensive care costs of perhaps £100,000 or £200,000, ends up not having to pay those care costs because they are capped'.

Nevertheless, the subsequent Queen's Speech omitted several policies touted in the Conservative election campaign, including the so-called 'dementia tax'. Instead the issue was ducked. Ministers are to consult on reforming the system of social care funding in England after effectively abandoning the controversial changes set out in the Conservative General Election manifesto. But it offered no specific proposals for change, and simply promised to 'work with partners at all levels' and to 'consult on options to encourage a wider debate'. A type of dishonesty writ large!

Inequality

Democracy is jeopardised by inequality when it concentrates power in the hands of the few and unleashes a market in political influence (Raworth, 2017). Grayling defines representative democracy as rule by elective representatives where the people (strictly: the enfranchised section of the populace) are the ultimate source of political and governmental legitimacy because a majority of their votes will endorse a legislature and executive, and by the same token can dismiss them, in terms of a structure in which the expression of this endorsement or withdrawal of endorsement is periodic and follows recognised and agreed processes (Grayling, 2017). Has it worked? The answer is arguably an only slightly qualified NO! Dissatisfaction that the peoples in democracies feel towards democracy has emerged in recent years as populism – the polar opposite of elitism. It is prompted by the feeling that governments are too remote and too unresponsive to concerns at the grassroots level and has allowed unacceptable inequality to develop.

Higher levels of national inequality, it turns out, also go hand in hand with increased ecological degradation. Inequality erodes social capital that underpins the collective action needed to demand, enact and enforce environmental legislation. Economic stability is jeopardised when resources become concentrated in too few hands. Both 1929 and 2008 saw a large increase in the income share of the rich, a fast-growing financial sector, and a large increase in the indebtedness of the rest of the population – culminating in financial and social crises.

In an ideal democracy, a well-informed populace deliberates about the common good and carefully selects leaders who carry out their preferences efficiently. By that standard, the number of democracies in the world was zero and still is zero. Political scientists are repeatedly astonished by the shallowness and incoherence of people's political beliefs, and by the tenuous connection of their preferences to their votes and to the behaviour of their representatives. If neither voters nor elected leaders can be counted on to uphold the ideals of democracy, why should this form of government work out not so badly? Well, democracy, John Mueller (political scientist, Ohio State University) suggests, is essentially based on giving people the freedom to complain and replace leadership non-violently. People with guns (the army) have to think that democracy is better than alternatives such as theocracy, the divine right of kings, colonial paternalism, the dictatorship of the proletariat, or authoritarian rule by a charismatic leader (Mueller, 2010).

People are getting not just healthier, richer, and safer, but freer. People recognise that democracies are relatively nice places to live. Two centuries ago only a handful of countries, embracing one per cent of the world's people, were democratic; today two thirds of the world's countries, embracing two thirds of its people, are. Not long ago half the world's countries had laws that discriminated against racial minorities; today more countries have policies that favour their minorities than policies that discriminate against them. At the turn of the twentieth century women could vote in just New Zealand; today they can vote in every country where men can vote, save one (Vatican City). Pinker wants to be positive about the progress democracies have helped bring about:

For all the bleeding headlines, for all the crises, collapses, scandals, plagues, epidemics, and existential threats, these are accomplishments to savour. The Enlightenment is working: for two and a half centuries, people have used knowledge to enhance human flourishing. Scientists have exposed the workings of matter, life and mind. Inventors have harnessed the laws of nature to defy entropy, and entrepreneurs have made their innovations affordable. Law-makers have made people better off by discouraging acts that are individually beneficial but collectively harmful. Diplomats have done the same with nations. Scholars have perpetuated the treasury of knowledge and augmented the power of reason. Artists have expanded the circle of sympathy. Activists have pressured the powerful to overturn repressive measures and their fellow citizens to change repressive norms. All these efforts have been channelled into institutions that have allowed us to circumvent some of the flaws of human nature (Pinker, 2018).

At the same time, over 800 million people in the world today live in extreme poverty (on an income of less than $1.80 per day, to take one definition, although Hickel, as we know, would set the international poverty line much higher!) In the regions where the extreme poor are concentrated, life expectancy is less than sixty years, and almost a quarter of the people are undernourished. Almost a million children die of pneumonia every year, half a million from diarrhoea or malaria, and hundreds of thousands from measles and AIDS. A dozen wars are raging in the world, including one in which more than 250,000 people have died, and in 2015 at least 10,000 people were slaughtered in genocides. More than two billion people, almost a third of humanity, are oppressed in autocratic states. Almost a fifth of the world's people lack a basic education; almost a sixth are illiterate. Every year five million people are killed in accidents, and more than 400,000 are murdered. Almost 300 million people in the world are clinically depressed, of whom almost 800,000 will die by suicide this year (Pinker, 2018).

And contrary to founding theories, inequality does not make economies grow faster: if anything, it slows them down by wasting the potential of much of the population. Many people have to spend their time desperately trying to meet their family's most basic needs. The market stagnates among those who need its dynamism most. Inequality undercuts GDP growth, for those who still believe in and want growth. It is a mistake to imagine that we can focus on economic growth and let inequality take care of itself. This is a powerful message for low- and middle-income countries and one that clearly contradicts the 'no pain, no gain' myth of the Kuznets curve.

The new message that decision makers must confront is simple:

> *Don't wait for economic growth to reduce inequality – because it won't. Instead, create an economy that is distributive by design. (Raworth, 2017)*

Such an economy must help to bring everyone above the Doughnut's social foundation. To do so, however, it must alter the distribution not only of income but also of wealth, time and power. Structuring an economy as a distributed network can more equitably distribute the income and wealth that it generates. Nature's thriving networks teach that success is found in diversity and distribution. Economic networks must distribute all value – from materials and energy to knowledge and income – in a far more equitable way (Raworth, 2017).

Planning economic policy to suit narrow nationalistic interests is no longer good enough. A much broader and wiser plan is needed from national and international organisations looking years and decades ahead. King recognises that such a plan is important. He focuses on macroeconomics. Setting interest rates and fixing the supply of money are closely related. If money supply was to expand at a rate much faster than the ability of the economy to grow, then the result would be inflation. Since most money comprises bank deposits, a fall in deposits means that the amount of money available to finance spending actually falls, threatening a depression. One method used by central banks to create more money for investment was purchasing large quantities of assets from the private sector – the practice known as unconventional monetary policy or 'quantitative easing' (King, 2016). Using such monies for long-term development has much to commend it. Hydroponics has long been developed in many poorly resourced countries. For example, in Egypt, funding new technologies to grow lettuce on trestles fed by nutrient-enhanced water in the warm climate is the type of investment that will help to reduce the need for food imports. Egypt is one of the largest importers of food in the world.

King also recognises, of course, in a world of radical uncertainty it is never clear whether a bank is solvent or insolvent and in a crisis there is rarely time to find out. Checks and balances are needed. Actions by a lender of last resort (LOLR – a central bank) can prevent a liquidity problem turning into a solvency problem, although not all solvency problems can be converted into liquidity problems by LOLR lending, as governments have painfully discovered in recent times. But the concept of 'emergency money' is important. It captures the need for a sudden increase in money when there is a sharp rise in the demand for liquidity (King, 2016).

With checks and balances in place, the need to treat bank executives as some sort of modern-day deities will disappear. Excessive share options and remuneration packages for those at the top of these organisations should disappear also. Of course all jobs should be respected, but some high earners (e.g. sports stars and business executives) need to have their earnings greatly reduced; public sector employees (e.g. doctors, lawyers and accountants) need to have their earnings reassessed, and there should be a much smaller standard deviation of pay around the mean to make societies more equal. There is much to be done in levelling out remuneration across the employment spectrum in all countries. The idea of having a maximum ratio of pay between the CEO and the bottom rungs of employees is a good one, e.g. 20:1. Again, a progressive wealth tax is needed ($r > g$) which could be used to set up national sovereign wealth funds and a global fund for a universal basic income. Market economies need to mature in new ways. Past market failures have led to highly fractured societies.

Although central banks have matured, they have not yet reached old age. Central banks have a role to play in changing the heuristics (allowing someone to learn something for themselves) used by households and businesses when they see serious disequilibrium building up. The freedom of a central bank to act in a crisis depends on its legitimacy, which requires a clear mandate of delegated powers from the legislature. Democratic legitimacy works at a national level. It is far from clear, however, that any democratic mandate can function at a supranational level (King, 2016). This is a core problem with the European Union and other trading blocs. Many decisions made at this level (adversely affecting nations inside the bloc and especially nations outside the bloc) are difficult for populations to control. '**Everything but Arms (EBA)** is an initiative of the European Union under which all imports to the EU from the Least Developed Countries are duty-free and quota-free, with the exception of armaments. EBA entered into force on 5 March 2001. There were transitional arrangements for bananas, sugar and rice until January 2006, July 2009 and September 2009 respectively. The EBA is part of the EU Generalised System of Preferences (GSP). The aim of the scheme is to encourage the development of the world's poorest countries but in fact, in the small print, there are tiered tariffs in place. It is all actually controlled and dictated by the EU for the benefit of Europeans to the detriment of developing nations. How much better it would have been if the EU had put each of its directives firstly through a 'sieve' to assess the impact on the 'have-nots' of the whole world.' (Wikipedia, 2018).

The attempt to break the link between money and nations has always been fraught with difficulty. Yanis Varoufakis, the former Greek finance minister, knows this only too well. Only a sovereign people can create political authority, whereas the Eurozone, an alliance of independently sovereign states, cannot. While the members of the European Council and the 'Eurogroup' are elected politicians, answerable to their respective national parliaments, the Council and Eurogroup themselves are not answerable to any public body whatsoever. The Eurogroup does not even exist in European Law; it operates on the basis that the *strong do as they please while the weak suffer what they must*' (Thucydides, Peloponnesian War, 404BC); it keeps no minutes, and all its deliberations are confidential – not to be shared with Europe's citizenry. Little redistribution takes place across Europe as a result (Varoufakis, 2016). A major issue for alternative strategies is moving beyond the nation state: central banks, national accounting offices, and currencies that separate people all are yesterday's solutions. A reinvigorated United

Nations as an effective supranational decision maker is essential.

The UN has six main divisions: the General Assembly, the Security Council, the Economic and Social Council (special agencies include UNESCO, WHO, World Bank), the Trusteeship Council, the International Court of Justice and the Secretariat. Current total funding for the UN exceeds $50 billion. The 2012 breakdown of contributions was approximately: USA 22%, Japan 9.6%, China 7.9%, France 4.8%, UK 4.4% and Russia 4.0%. At present there are 193 members. Carne Ross, who has worked at the UN, acknowledged on *The Moral Maze* (BBC Radio 4, 21 November 2018) that there is no shortage of people quick with their criticism of the UN. Its record on conflict resolution is poor. The Security Council's independence is questioned because of the frequent use of vetoes by its permanent members as they navigate around the geopolitical playground. He feels that the UN respects sovereignty too much and should allow greater agency to those lacking a voice in the world – refugees, for example. An idea for reform might be a world parliament with representatives directly elected by populations rather than nominated by governments. The case for a world parliament has been examined in considerable compelling detail by Monbiot (2003) in *The Age of Consent*. Manifestos for such elections would be invigorated by the new world parliament being given control over a universal basic income fund of $25–30 trillion, as previously outlined. In time this should see a useful shift of power away from the Security Council and lead to more democracy everywhere. Monbiot, writing again in *The Guardian* in 2007 about the need for a world parliament, observed:

> *No political issue now stops at the national border. All the most important forces – climate change, terrorism, state aggression, trade, flows of money, demographic pressures, the depletion of resources – can be addressed only at the global level. The question is not whether global decisions need to be made. The question is how to ensure that they are made democratically. Is there any valid answer other than direct representation in a world parliament? Global democracy has a special problem – the scale on which it must operate. The bigger the electorate, the less democratic a parliamentary body will be. True democracy could exist only in the village, where representatives are subject to constant oversight by their electorate. But an imperfect system is better than no system at all, and a world parliament would be the best way to give the poor a voice and bypass corruption (Monbiot, 2007).*

Corruption

We should pause for a moment and consider the role of corruption in some detail. Transparency International and its global map of degrees of corruption were mentioned above. It is a global coalition against corruption, which publishes a 'Corruption Perceptions Index'. The latest figures are for 2016. Let's get straight to the point: no country gets close to a perfect score in the Corruption Perceptions Index 2016. Over two thirds of the 176 countries and territories in that year's index fall below the midpoint of the scale: 0 (highly corrupt) to 100 (very clean). The global average score is a paltry 43, indicating endemic corruption in a country's public sector. Top-scoring countries are far outnumbered by countries where citizens face the tangible impact of corruption on a daily basis. But corruption hurts all countries, in every region of the world. Top of the index was Denmark (score 90), followed by New Zealand and more Scandinavian countries, UK (81), and USA (74). Greece (44) is one of the worst European countries. And Peter Rookes' heavily studied pair – India (40) and Malawi (31) – did not fare well, but bottom of the pile was Somalia (10).

That year's results highlight the **connection between corruption and inequality**, which feed off each other to create a vicious circle. Corruption leads to the unequal distribution of power in society, and then to the unequal distribution of wealth which encourages more corruption. 'In too many countries, people are deprived of their most basic needs and go to bed hungry every night in part because of corruption, while the powerful and corrupt enjoy lavish lifestyles with impunity', says José Ugaz, Chair of Transparency International.

The interplay of corruption and inequality (or at least the link in people's minds) also feeds our old friend populism. When traditional politicians fail to tackle corruption, people grow cynical. Increasingly, people are turning to populist leaders who promise to break the cycle of corruption and privilege. Yet this is likely to exacerbate – rather than resolve – the tensions that fed the populist surge in the first place. More countries worsened rather than improved their Corruption Perceptions Index in 2016, showing the urgent need for committed action to thwart corruption.

The **lower-ranked countries** in the index are plagued by untrustworthy and badly functioning public institutions like the police and judiciary. Even where anti-corruption laws are on the books, in practice they're often skirted or ignored. People frequently face situations of bribery and extortion, rely on basic services that have been undermined by the misappropriation of funds, and confront official indifference when seeking redress from authorities that are on the take. Corruption thrives in such settings and collusion between businesses and politicians siphons off revenue from national economies, benefitting the few at the expense of the many. This kind of systemic grand corruption violates human rights, prevents sustainable development and fuels social exclusion. On the other hand, Sachs does some myth busting in *The End of Poverty*. Back in 2005, he opened one of his concluding chapters by stating that:

> 'Africa needs around $30 billion per year in aid to escape from poverty. But if we actually gave that aid, where would it go? Right down the drain if the past is any guide. Sad to say, Africa's education levels are so low that even programs that work elsewhere would fail in Africa. Africa is corrupt and riddled with authoritarianism. It lacks modern values and the institutions of a free market economy needed to achieve success. In fact, African morals are so broken down that it is no surprise AIDS has run out of control. And here is the bleakest truth: Suppose that our aid saved Africa's children. What then? There would be a population explosion, and a lot more hungry adults. We would have solved nothing' (Sachs, 2005).

However, while commonly heard, these assertions are totally incorrect. Why have these prejudices become accepted truths? Alldred's personal experience of twenty-five years in Africa confirms that there was myriad petty corruption but the really serious stuff was entirely facilitated by Western governments and corporations (Alldred, personal communication, 2018). London and other major Western cities bend over backwards to allow residency for former dictators and their families, provided they have the money.

Higher-ranked countries tend to have higher degrees of press freedom, access to information about public expenditure, stronger standards of integrity for public officials, and independent judicial systems. But high-scoring countries can't afford to be complacent, either. While the most obvious forms of corruption may not scar citizens' daily lives in all these places, the higher-ranked countries are not immune to closed-door deals, conflicts of interest, illicit finance, and patchy law enforcement that can distort public policy and exacerbate corruption at home and abroad. And when it comes to charges of bad governance, the West should be a little more circumspect. Little surpasses the Western world in the cruelty and depredations that it has long imposed on Africa. Apart from slavery, borders drawn arbitrarily divided ethnic groups, ecosystems, watersheds and resource deposits. Even in the 1980s and 1990s, Western governments enforced draconian budget policies in Africa and elsewhere via the IMF (Sachs, 2005). Everyone needs to remember that every day the greatest corruption is the vast flow of monies from the Global South into Western banks in debt repayments, income extraction by foreign investors and capital flight (Hickel, 2017).

Technology

Jamie Bartlett (the former Director of the Centre for Analysis of Social Media for DEMOS), in his 2018 book *The People Vs Tech* , sees technology as posing major threats to democracy. Information overload and connectivity has encouraged a divisive form of emotional tribal politics, in which loyalty to the group and anger outrank reason and compromise. While partisanship is necessary in politics, too much of it is dangerous. Political leaders are evolving their approach to the new medium of information – hence the rise of populists who promise emotional, immediate and total answers. But warring tribes of anchorless, confused citizens are a precursor to totalitarianism (Bartlett, 2018).

To really make national economies regenerative and distributive, democratic legitimacy is important. What is the role of 'fake news' and 'populism'? Though closely intertwined, we will consider populism first. Populism is dangerous simply because it is essentially a self-centred and selfish phenomenon. Some of the recent upsurge in populism is undoubtedly because the 2008 financial crisis marked the end of the dominant consensus in favour of economic and political liberalisation, shifting political energy towards populist extremes. Populism leads variously to revolution at one end of the spectrum, or to surprise outcomes in elections at the other, for example the Arab Spring, Brexit and the Trump phenomenon. It does not add any extra democratic legitimacy. At a time when it should be vital to take a global view of the great issues affecting the world, particularly in regard to reducing inequality and ecological damage, to have nations such as the USA considering protectionism is especially dangerous.

Jamie Bartlett points out that we are living through a great re-tribalisation of politics. It is re-tribalisation because tribal loyalties and identity have characterised human existence for far longer than modern politics. We've had enough civil wars to know that the need to belong to a group is deep-rooted. Crowds certainly are wise when it comes to solving technical, on-value based problems, like fixing computer bugs, but political and moral decision making is very different. The 'global village' has inadvertently let tribalism back out of the cage that modern representative democracy built for it. Although it could be said that at least the 'global village' has shed some light into dark corners of tribal backwardness, for example female genital mutilation.

Flimsy news

One of the most important – and sudden – changes in politics for several decades has been the move from a world of information scarcity to one of overload. The basis of what this is doing to politics is now fairly well-trodden stuff: the splintering of established mainstream news and a surge of misinformation allows people to personalise their sources in ways that play to their pre-existing biases. Faced with infinite connections, we find the like-minded people and ideas, and huddle together in 'filter bubbles' and 'echo chambers'. Digital communication is changing the very nature of how we engage with political ideas and how we understand ourselves as political actors. Political theorists call this re-tribalisation 'identity politics'. The Internet is the largest vehicle of tribal grievances in the history of mankind (Bartlett, 2018). It must be remembered that humanity has been tribal for countless millennia and only in the last hundred years or so have there been some tentative experiments in global cooperation instead, firstly the League of Nations and then the United Nations. We need to define 'we' carefully and correctly. Montesquieu countered against tribalism over 300 years ago: '*Si je savais une chose utile à ma nation qui fût ruineuse à une autre, je ne la proposerais pas à mon prince, parce que je suis homme avant d'être Français, parce que je suis nécessairement homme, et que je ne suis Français que par hasard*' – translated: 'If I knew of something that could serve my nation but would ruin another, I would not propose it to my prince, for I am first a man and only then a Frenchman, because I am necessarily a man, and only accidentally am I French'.

The promotion of cooperation and functioning global institutions is going to be very important. Part of the problem is how poorly informed many populations are; or more strictly correct would be to say how superficially issues have been analysed by people who think they are well informed by the Internet and the global communications revolution. 'Fake news' (or economies with the truth) is one thing but 'flimsy news' (poor reporting of and the lack of linking together global issues by previously reputable news organisations) is also widespread. If people cannot grasp that global gross inequality and its complexities are at the root of many of the world's problems (poverty, terrorism, mass migration, environmental damage), is it surprising that they then make bad choices and turn to the 'demagogues'? Raphaël Liogier (French sociologist and philosopher) feels populism should not be confused with demagoguery; rather, it claims to express the emotions of the people who feel they are losing their identity. There are those who extol populism as an authentic expression of democracy, but it is the element in which demagogues swim. The immediate takes precedence over the long-term, localism obscures the bigger picture, and parochial attitudes drown out carefully worked through ideas (Liogier, 2017). So the kinds of reasons John Stuart Mill had for espousing plural voting reappear here, as the ochlocratic spectre (rule of the mob) arises in connection with direct democracy, popular feeling, increasing xenophobia and intolerant nationalism generally.

Over the years, Bartlett's optimism about technology drifted into realism, and then morphed into nervousness. Now it is approaching mild panic. Democracy is analogue (reacting to change slowly) rather than digital (reacting to change quickly). And any vision of the future that runs contrary to the reality of people's lives and wishes can only end in disaster.

He feels that we live in a giant advertising panopticon which keeps us addicted to devices. This system of data collection and prediction is merely the most recent iteration in a long history of efforts to control us; it is getting more advanced by the day, which has serious ramifications for potential manipulation, endless distraction and the slow diminishing of free choice and autonomy.

Algorithms

American psychology has looked at how to turn the question of human decision making into a hard science that could be used by business. Sean Parker, Facebook's first president, recently called the 'like' button 'a social-validation feedback loop … exactly the kind of thing that a hacker would come up with, because you are exploiting a vulnerability in human psychology'. (Huddleson Jnr, 2017; Bartlett, 2018).

The data windfall is far beyond human analysis these days, which is why algorithms have become so central to the modern economy. Algorithms are the magic keys to the kingdom, which filter, predict, correlate, target and learn. The scary thing about modern big data algorithms is how they can figure things out about us that we barely know ourselves. The logical end goal of dataism is for each of us to be reduced to a unique, predictable and targetable data point.

However, this whole pattern that leads from data collection, to analysis, to prediction, to targeting, presents three challenges to the life of a democratic citizen. The first is the question of whether being under the glare of social media and constant data collection allows people to mature politically. The second is the danger that these tools are used to manipulate, distract and influence us in ways that are not in our best interests. The third is more hypothetical and existential: the concern about whether we even trust ourselves to make important moral decisions at all.

Our critical faculties only improve through the repeated use of reason, evidence and moral inquisition. It is not easy to develop these critical faculties, but it is the duty of every citizen fortunate enough to live in a democracy to do so. As algorithms get faster and smarter, the pressure will grow to hand these inconveniences over for the sake of ease, speed or ignorance. To give in to this urge would be easy, but it would condemn us to losing the ability to think freely, and to spiral into ever greater reliance on machines. Given how bad we often are at making difficult decisions, the result might be a wiser and more humane society. But Bartlett feels it would be difficult to call such a place a democracy (Bartlett, 2018).

Freedom and truth

How can representative democracy combat these problems? Grayling believes there are three main reasons why representative democracy has failed to deliver on the promise of its design. The first failure is because those who take control deliberately redirect the democratic process in ways more convenient for the practice of government and party-political interests. The second is the failure to equip the *demos* for their part in the process, for example, with poor civic education and flimsy news. The third is interference and manipulation by agencies with partisan interests who recognise that they are unlikely to get their interests favoured otherwise, for example big business and party donors.

His suggested remedies include the following:

1. There should be complete transparency about individuals and organisations involved in elections
2. There should be complete transparency about the funding involved in an election campaign
3. The press should be subject to strict fact-check monitoring
4. Betting on the outcome of elections should be banned
5. Voting should be compulsory for all citizens, along with civic education
6. An adequate proportional representation system is essential
7. Reform of party discipline system with limited whipping only on manifesto commitments (Grayling, 2017).

Despite the problems with representative democracy, and the mistakes of the past outlined by Cocker, there are defenders of Western democratic culture, such as historian Niall Ferguson and former Deputy Australian Prime Minister John Anderson. They point to the emphasis on freedom of speech and the search for truth as attitudes worth defending because they are rooted in the Judaeo-Christian tradition.

Supranational institutions

King quotes Wolfgang Schäuble, former German finance minister, 2015: 'Elections change nothing. There are rules'. And it could be added that elections change nothing if election manifestos break the bounds of common economic sense.

Would the collapse of the European Union be a blessing in disguise? Viewed from many parts of the world, the European Union must be seen as a morally dubious organisation. It is basically a closed cartel setting up a wall of tariffs against some of the poorest nations on Earth who desperately need to trade their way out of debt. Fair trade is needed to give the real poorest of the world a fair chance.

Varoufakis has annoyed just about everyone in European politics. He correctly identifies that the European Union began as a protective cartel of coal and steel producers designed to shore up elites. Technocracy, he says, led from Platonic contempt for democracy to antisocial autocracy. He seems to largely skim over the corruption and political incompetence that led to the problems facing his own country, Greece. Yet he clearly points out questions about the lack of sovereignty (hence 'taking back control'). Others seem trapped in a 'little European bubble', unable to take a worldwide view, and therefore they miss the damage that institutions like the EU inflict on millions of poor people outside Europe (Varoufakis, 2017). The correct focus should be on supranational institutions which could take a global viewpoint such as a reformed United Nations and a world parliament.

Aid

Since 2000, global income inequality has narrowed slightly, largely due to poverty reduction in China. But the world as a whole remains more unequal than any single country within it. The history of overseas development aid's rich-to-poor transfers is nothing short of a myopic failure in global action. Much less has been given than was pledged – that missing finance would have empowered women, transformed livelihoods, boosted prosperity and stabilised the global population. Instead global migrants have stepped in –

sending monies back home that currently outstrip all overseas development aid put together.

High-income countries complain that much aid gets embezzled by corrupt leaders or wasted on poorly designed projects, as discussed earlier. Certainly all the aid poured in over recent years, particularly to Africa, has shown poor results. What if all overseas development aid was channelled directly to people living in poverty as a basic income? Mobile banking could make this work (the M-Pesa in Kenya again as viable avenue), but it also must be acknowledged that private incomes are no substitute for public services. The market works best in tackling inequality when it complements the state and commons.

The Western world spends $4,274 a second on foreign development aid (although twice as much is spent on subsidising domestic agriculture). Nobody knows if it helps. Bizarrely, the first randomised control trial of foreign development aid did not happen until 1998. Professor Michael Kremer (Professor of Philosophy, University of Chicago) showed that supplying free textbooks to Kenyan grade-school pupils made no difference to test scores. Also in Kenya, it was discovered that people who previously received free mosquito nets to prevent malaria proved twice as likely to purchase a new net as those who paid £3 the first time around. Doing randomised controlled trials in poverty-stricken countries is difficult, time consuming and expensive. But an Randomised Controlled Trial (RCT) in Hyderabad, India showed no hard evidence that microcredit is effective in combating poverty and illness; rather handing out cash works way better. Thanks to RCTs, we know that £100 worth of free school meals translates into three times more educational attainment than free uniforms, and cheaply deworming children yields much additional school time.

Professor Esther Duflo, MIT, calls the three I's of development aid – Ideology, Ignorance and Inertia. But RCTs cannot answer everything. The OECD estimates that poor countries lose three times as much to tax evasion as they receive in foreign aid. Measures against tax havens, for example, could potentially do far more good than well-meaning aid programs ever could. On an even bigger scale, open borders (for people and goods) would be the most effective strategy, making the whole world perhaps twice as rich. We should throw open the gates of the Land of Plenty. (Bregman, 2018).

Open borders

The world's borders were still as good as open only a century ago. Passports are new. In this era of 'globalisation', only three per cent of the world's population lives outside their country of birth. Oddly though, the world is pretty wide open for everything but people. Sure, we have trade barriers, but even if we scrapped them the global economy would only grow by a few percentage points. With free movement of people wealth would be boosted a thousand times more ($65 trillion perhaps) (Bregman, 2018).

> 'Out beyond the gates of the Land of Plenty, economic growth is still the driver of progress. Billions of people are forced to sell their labour at a fraction of the price they would get in the developed world, all because of borders – the single biggest cause of discrimination in all of world history' (Bregman, 2018).

The reason for an absence of multilateral institutions overseeing labour and migration is obvious: the rich and powerful countries have no interest in raising the issues. It is the binary nature of citizenship that makes the citizenship of rich countries very valuable. There is a huge financial wall around rich countries. This financial wall could be lowered through the introduction of an intermediate level of citizenship (higher taxes and lower access to social services). But is this ethical? Fully open and free movement of people would be a simpler and better solution. Three obvious drawbacks that are raised are: (1) population density – if millions more arrived in an already cramped Holland, it would create a great deal of tension, to say the least; (2) cultural conflicts – the large-scale movement of people from one culture into another does present genuine difficulties of assimilation, many of which Holland and other European countries are already contending with; (3) brain drain - if it is the better-off in poorer countries who are most likely to leave, it robs those nations of a much-needed middle class which stifles Third World development (Bregman, 2017). Any changes in the near future are unlikely to lead immediately to fully open borders so the development of poor nations will remain of crucial importance (Milanovic, 2016). We will look in more detail at how this development might be achieved in an ecologically sustainable manner in Chapter 8.

Combating pessimism
Perhaps these ideas of a universal basic income, a global knowledge commons and open borders, if implemented by decision makers worldwide, would go some way to dispelling Kingsnorth's depressive vision of the future and provide some alternatives to his rather gloomy personal action plan:

Over the next few years, the old green movement is likely to fall to pieces as it refuses to speak up for a subjective, non-technical engagement with nature. The neo-environmentalists have a great advantage over the old greens (with their threatening talk about limits to growth, behaviour change and other such against-the-grain stuff): rather the neo-environmentalists are telling this civilisation what it wants to hear – the progress trap can be escaped from in a green tech bubble. (Kingsnorth, 2017).

Pinker believes that the spectre of a population explosion has now vanished. Global population increase will 'probably' fall to zero by 2070, partly because of better-educated women and better food production. He trusts that science will come up with carbon-free energy sources (hypothetical nuclear fusion reactors that consume their own waste), which will allow desalination of the oceans (Carey, 2018). Alldred has long campaigned for major solar-powered desalination plants along the West Coast of Africa (Senegal, Mauritania and Western Sahara) to power two major canals across the Sahara as far as Central Chad (Alldred, personal communication, 2018).

Kingsnorth continues:

> In the long term the neo-environmentalists will fail for two reasons. Firstly, because bubbles always burst. Our civilisation is beginning to break down, with gradual economic and social collapse amongst background planetary ecocide, which nobody seems able to prevent. Secondly, it will be unlikely the new world they want to see can be built. Our human relationship with nature is a complex love–hate one. We are not headed towards human-scale development … I am very pessimistic about the near future. I bet on a strange and unworldly combination of an on-going collapse that will continue to fragment both nature and culture, and a new wave of techno-green 'solutions' being unveiled in a doomed attempt to prevent it. Nothing can break this cycle, bar some kind of reset: the kind we have seen many times in human history. Some kind of fall back down to a lower level of civilisational complexity (Kingsnorth, 2017).

Kingsnorth wants to be honest about where we are in history's great cycle and what we have the power to do and not do. In asking what would not be a waste of time and he comes up with five tentative personal answers:

1. **Withdrawing.** People will say 'fighting' is always better than 'quitting'. But withdrawing and refusing to help the 'machine' advance in tightening the ecologically destructive ratchet further and carefully examining

your worldview is a deeply moral position. All real change starts with withdrawal. Should one fly across the world on holiday?

2. **Preserving non-human life.** Maybe you can buy up some land and re-wild it; maybe you can let your garden run free; maybe you can work for a conservation group; maybe you can use your skills to prevent the destruction of yet another wild place, for example: www.theoceancleanup.com and the fight against plastic polluting our oceans.

3. **Getting your hands dirty.** Root yourself in something: some practical work, some place, and some way of doing. Do physical work in clean air surrounded by things you cannot control.

4. **Insisting that nature has a value beyond utility.** Understand that everything has intrinsic value. Value it for what it is, try to understand what it is, and have nothing but pity or contempt for people who tell you that its only value is in what they can extract from it.

5. **Building refuges.** Advanced technologies will challenge our sense of what it means to be human at the same time as the tide of extinction rolls on. Can you work to create places or networks that act as refuges from the unfolding storm? Can you act like the librarian of a monastery through the Dark Ages, guarding the old books as empires rise and fall outside? (Kingsnorth, 2017)

But if you take Kingsnorth's claims seriously, you'll want conclusions with more 'oomph'. It's easy to see why Kingsnorth's critics call him a defeatist. However, his pessimism should not mute his call for something stronger than carbon taxes and whatever other technofuturist solutions are currently being imagined as band-aids. It is a pathological worldview that considers humans and the environment to be separable. Perhaps there is an important role for online campaigning organisations, such as change.org and 38degrees.org.uk, to crowd-source opinion in support of grassroots pressure groups which can help influence decision makers in good democratic directions. There may have been a time when engaging in resistance against a life-threatening system and building alternatives to that system could be meaningfully separated, but today we have to do both. Dropping out and planting vegetables in Galway, à la Paul Kingsnorth, is not an option for this generation (Klein, 2014).

Stiglitz wants to make some suggestions to combat the international financial instability that causes such damage among the 'have-nots' and those who have been the losers in globalisation. The international community could provide a new form of fiat money to act as reserves (Stiglitz – 'global greenbacks'), which could be exchanged for local currencies in a time of crisis. There should be a tax levied on countries running a trade surplus, to discourage them from letting the trade surplus grow too large. The United States might think that the 'global greenbacks reserve system' would make it worse off because it would no longer effectively get cheap loans from developing countries. There is, of course, something unseemly about the poorest countries providing low-interest loans to the richest. And all would benefit from greater global stability (Stiglitz, 2006).

Creating a global knowledge commons and open borders are also immediately positive and feasible. And a dedicated global digital platform enabling innovators worldwide to collaborate with researchers, students, enterprises and NGOs to develop open-source technologies would be a start. This needs start-up funding and new forms of open-source licensing to allow the resurgent knowledge commons to flourish and everyone to make better decisions.

In summary, most would agree with Jamie Bartlett and A C Grayling that good decision making depends on a blend of different things: alert, independent-minded citizens who are capable of making important moral judgements; a democratic culture which rests on a commonly agreed reality, a shared identity and a spirit of compromise; elections that are free, fair and trusted; manageable levels of equality, including a sizeable middle class; a competitive economy and an independent civil society; and finally, a sovereign authority that can enforce the people's will, but remains trustworthy and accountable to them (Bartlett, 2018). This is not applicable to the nation state only.

CHAPTER 8

BEING SYMPATHETIC TO NATURE AND HUMANITY

RETURNING TO OUR TWO existential threats (inequality and ecological damage), there are some other issues that will have influence in the very near future. These issues, especially concerning morality, need to be considered before turning to some solutions.

It is said that there were many different reasons for a Brexit vote in the UK European Referendum in 2016; some may have voted because of high levels of immigration, some because of a dislike of EU bureaucracy or some simply 'to take back control', as mentioned previously. A vote for Malawi was an extremely uncommon reason for voting in the UK European Referendum. I 'voted for Malawi' by voting to leave the EU, because I believe the EU is ethically not the right type of supranational institution for the next few critical decades. A vote for the Third World, within a referendum ostensibly about Europe, was part of an alternative way of looking at things. We need better supranational structures that serve the needs of all peoples. It must be remembered that in a still deeply unequal world, it's not all about us.

Narcissism

We live in a world of 'selfies', where every moment of our lives can be posted online for the world to see. It is easy to believe that everything of great import is, in the end, 'all about us'! Perhaps we would to do well to reflect on

Philippians 2:4: '*Let each of you look not to your own interests; but to the interests of others*'. How timely are these words of St Paul. The world of 'selfie-ness' begins and ends with the individual. Paul gives some simple alternative ideas – be an encouragement; offer support and sympathy to others. Can it be so simple? Well, of course things are not simple at all. There are many uncomfortable and challenging issues for the Western world to consider. Jonathan Sacks, the Chief Rabbi in the UK from 1991–2013, feels morality is our oldest and most powerful resource for turning disconnected 'I's into a collective 'we', and self-interested striving into empathy, sympathy and compassion for others. In recent broadcasts and writings, Lord Sacks examines how we have come to believe that you can outsource morality to the market and the state. But this only works in the short-term. In the long-term, when all that matters is wealth and power, the wealthy and powerful gain and the poor and the powerless suffer. Morality is about cooperation – it's the world of 'we' not 'I'. It is born and sustained in families, communities, voluntary organisations and religious congregations (Sacks, 2018).

> *Many nowadays have been brought up on a steady diet of narcissism, which conceals an ocean of uncertainty. Never before have so many young adults been seeing a psychiatrist nor have there been so many early career burnouts. Where our grandparents still toed the lines imposed by family, church and country, we're hemmed in by the media, marketing and a paternalistic state. It is capitalism that opened the gates to the Land of Plenty, but capitalism alone cannot sustain it. While young people in the West have largely come of age in an era of apolitical technocracy, we will have to return to politics and morality again to find a new utopia (Bregman, 2018).*

One side of *Oikos*

Firstly, we need to accept that there should be no first-class and no second-class human beings. Humanity is not divided, like football leagues, into the Premiership and First/Second/Third Divisions. Fair access to resources and opportunities for all should be the basic standards for ordering our affairs. The Ancient Greek concept of *oikos* has some relevance here – surely, ethically, we are all a family of equals, all in one home. The modern wave of populism sweeping through many countries is actually the complete opposite. Nations 'pulling up the drawbridge' to look after their own first is only going to reinforce inequality between the 'haves' and the 'have-nots'. It is shameful that within some countries there are even calls to **reduce** overseas aid funding (whether from 0.7% of GDP or another amount) to spend more at home! And not many of us in the UK have opened our doors to a Syrian refugee or their family. This may not be the answer for individual families (UK or foreign) looking for some privacy to settle in a new peaceful environment, but the Land of Plenty should still be trying to accommodate the displaced and dispossessed wherever possible.

Spending at home raises a **second** unsettling issue. The demands of modern healthcare and education can become black holes for funds. The political reality in the Western world is that it can become an irresistible temptation for those seeking election in democratic societies to promise the earth in terms of additional spending. Healthcare and education are, of course, things we should be aiming to increase spending on – but there must be limits. In office, politicians run up huge national debts to try and fulfil their manifestos. To try and stand, pre-election, on a more honest agenda of a balanced budget would be admitting that standards of living of the whole population have to change to a more sustainable level, and this currently would be political suicide. It certainly does not happen at present. But this poses a profound problem for democracies – if politicians who genuinely want to balance the books and introduce a fairer world order cannot get elected, then a 'me-first' agenda is going to continue to hold sway. This agenda has certainly taken the upper hand in the United States currently. As mentioned above, from a global perspective this is bad news for the Third World.

A **third**, allied problem is that the true appreciation of these issues among the general populations of many countries is low. If voters do not have the correct information and analyses of these issues, it is unrealistic to expect mature choices to be made. People who also feel they are struggling in comparison with their peers, in societies which are allowing internal inequalities to grow, will find it especially difficult to look beyond their own self-interest. It is easy for many heads to be buried in the sand or to exist within a little news/information bubble. If this bubble is made up of 'fake news', 'flimsy news' or opinion targeted to promote a sense of entitlement then it is especially dangerous. Even many mainstream journals do not seem to have analysed all the global issues accurately enough. Jason Brennan (an American philosopher and political scientist) believes that democracy can dis-incentivise people from acting wisely: since individual votes count for so little, each voter can afford to be ignorant and misinformed about politics and economics, or to indulge their worst biases and delusions (Brennan, 2016).

Fourthly, science fiction is fast becoming science fact, as rapidly improving artificial intelligence starts to impact our economy. However, rather than speculating about a 'jobless future', we should be worrying about growing inequality and whether the coming tech revolution will wipe out the middle class. In the second technological revolution, more jobs combine scalability with wide reach and so wage inequality tends to rise (Milanovic, 2016).

We should be reasonably confident that AI will result in forward leaps in productivity and overall wealth. The big question is how the spoils of that wealth will be shared out. The strange thing about the Western economy is that non-routine jobs tend to be either very well paid or very badly paid. If we lose the 'routine cognitive' jobs in the middle, we are heading for a barbell-shaped (or hour-glass) economy – a kind of extreme inequality. Those who can afford the best AI assistants will see their prospects rise further. In addition to favouring more skilled workers, digital technology also increases the financial returns to capital over labour. The unions' slow decline has been disastrous for wealth equality and new technology is likely to further militate against worker unionisation in the 'gig economy'. While some degree of inequality is inevitable and necessary in a free market economy, too much is bad for democracy. It is well documented that, up until now, a healthy democracy has depended on a vibrant, sizeable middle class. Maybe social classes, as we knew them over the last 200 years, have run their course and there will be different structures to contend with in the future?

So we return again to the idea of a universal basic income (UBI). For some on the political right, it is a way to keep capitalism ticking over in times of economic uncertainty. For some on the left, it represents a way to redistribute wealth more fairly. Bartlett feels it is an idea worth exploring but feels UBI would not stop a tiny band of elites from becoming even wealthier than everyone else. The dystopia we should fear is not robots taking all the jobs, but a barbell-shaped economy where socially progressive tech millionaires live in gated communities well away from the masses who they either fear, patronise or detest (Bartlett, 2018).

Relative and absolute poverty

With these issues preventing the development of a fairer world order is it any wonder many in the Third World are starting to vote with their feet? The wave of immigration of the 'have-nots' is certainly building momentum. Another paradoxical way to look at the Brexit vote would be 'all out, all in'. A nation taking *all out* control of its borders could simply institute an 'open doors' policy and allow *all in*. It is very difficult for the 'haves' to argue against this approach from a moral standpoint. Just because a particular country is blessed with huge natural resources or other advantages, it should not unilaterally elect itself to an elite league. Borders should be open – quotas or social engineering are not the answers. Those who want to start afresh elsewhere should be able to do so, but probably most people would prefer to make a real go of their lives in their homeland given a fair chance. To avoid the need for mass movements of people, with all the social upheaval that this entails, a fairer sharing of the resources and opportunities for each human being wherever they were born would be a better way forward. Very unsettling this may be for many people, but a 'vote for Malawi' is a positive vote.

Taking a positive view of the break-up of the European Union, as an opportunity for individual countries to each redesign their economies to a more redistributive and regenerative pattern, would hopefully lead to others following good practice. A balance has to be struck between obtaining meaningful change which all of a people buy into, within a cohesive nation state, and new economic pilot projects in different regions which may be destabilising to sovereign nations. The UK has undergone a gradual process of devolution over the last twenty years without an obvious move towards what Raworth would describe as a distributive and regenerative economy in any of its regions.

'Sterlingisation', for an independent Scotland, is a perfectly reasonable policy for a country that is happy to accept the economic consequences of a fixed exchange rate with sterling. But independence for Scotland was a question about political identity. The relationship between nations and their money reflects politics more than economics. And the same applies to the relationships between nations and their banks (King, 2016).

There is no absolute poverty in the UK, for example, as judged from the Third World perspective. Perhaps the 1.6 million Scots who voted for independence in 2014 would do well to take note that, viewed from Blantyre or Lilongwe (Malawi), the people of Easterhouse (Glasgow) and West Pilton (Edinburgh) are very well off and very lucky indeed just as they are right now! It is time for some real social justice. The Great Recession and the huge public debts that resulted from it sparked a sovereign debt crisis across Europe which has yet to be resolved. Let us, and the rest of Europe, pay off our debts first. The top ten per cent in these countries are the folk with necessary capital, much of which may be mobile, so again we return to a progressive global wealth tax. This will probably involve the break-up of the Eurozone and the European Union. The EU should not be a cosy club just looking after the interests of 'rich' (but actually publicly bankrupt) Europeans to the detriment of everyone else. People living in Scotland should be very cautious about any future constitutional decisions they make, especially if they have not got specific plans in place to make their new economy distributive and regenerative.

Designing regeneration
The people of Scotland and indeed the whole of modern civilisation have even more important ecological decisions to make right now. According to Kingsnorth in *Confessions of a Recovering Environmentalist*:

...We have imagined ourselves isolated from the source of our existence – nature. The fallout from this imaginative error is all around us: a quarter of the world's mammals are threatened with imminent extinction; an acre and a half of rainforest is felled every second; the world's oceans are full of plastic; 75 per cent of the world's fish stocks are on the verge of collapse; humanity consumes 25 per cent more of the world's natural 'products' faster than the Earth can replace. And over it all looms runaway climate change which threatens to render all human projects irrelevant (Kingsnorth, 2017).

Raworth's **sixth idea** optimistically attempts to address these environmental issues **by creating to regenerate – moving from 'growth will clean it up again' to regenerative by design**.

Just as economists debunked the Kuznets curve, its cousin, the similarly inverted U-shaped 'environmental Kuznets curve', entered centre stage – growth would clean up air and water pollution above $8,000 per capita mark. Advances in natural resource flow accounting data tell a very different story. When a nation's global material footprint (certainly a complex calculation) is taken into account the real environmental Kuznets curve rises and rises to a plateau, which is unfeasibly high. All countries cannot follow this path or the earth will be pushed into extreme overshoot beyond its planetary boundaries. The United Nations needs to lead radical change because countries switching to service industries just sends the heavy industries and pollutants overseas – eventually there will be nowhere left to outsource the pollution to!

In the meantime, remember:

- Citizens do not have to wait for growth to demand clean air and water
- Using 'people power' on governments and companies can compel industries to switch to cleaner technologies, growth or no growth (Raworth, 2017).

So is the environmental glass half full (Pinker) or half empty (Kingsnorth)? Pinker admits that there are environmental problems. The microscopic vantage point reveals pollutants that insidiously poison us; the macroscopic vantage point reveals effects on ecosystems which build up to tragic degradation and climate change. But he champions the new environmental movement, which he calls 'ecomodernism'. He begins with the assertion that 'some degree of pollution is an inescapable consequence of the Second Law of Thermodynamics' (total entropy of a closed system can never decrease over time). However, this predisposes a linear caterpillar type of economy of degenerative industrial design – take, make, use, lose. A better model would be a circular butterfly regenerative economy where the end 'waste' product of one process becomes the substrate for the next regenerative process.

William Cronon (Frederick Jackson Turner and Vilas Research Professor of History, Geography and Environmental Studies, University of Wisconsin) writes that 'wilderness' is not a pristine sanctuary; it is itself a product of civilisation (Cronon, 1995). 'Natural farming' is a contradiction in terms. Ecomodernism contends that industrialisation has been good for humanity and the trade-off that pits human well-being against environmental damage can be renegotiated by technology. Pinker blames ecopessimists for dismissing the hope that technology will transform the situation and for prophecies of environmental doomsdays that have never happened.

> 'The evidence is that the "population bomb" is being defused. So far resources refuse to run out. Instead, as the most easily extracted supply of a resource becomes scarcer, its price rises, encouraging conservation or more plentiful/better alternatives. The Stone Age did not run out of stones. Carbon-free energy sources could, as mentioned earlier, allow the desalination of seawater in the future, for example' (Pinker, 2018).

Though tropical forests are still, alarmingly, being cut down, the rate of deforestation of the Brazilian Amazon peaked in 2004 and has fallen slightly since, although this progress was stalling in 2018. All but two indicators on the Environmental Performance Index have shown an improvement. The wealthier the country, on average, the cleaner its environment. Poverty is a great polluter. The rural poor of Ethiopia may produce very little emissions (mainly a little smoke from firewood), whereas life in the UK produces about ten tonnes of CO_2 per person, but also in the reckoning is the large amount of plastic entering the oceans from the great rivers of Asia.

> 'Conservation experts are unanimous in their assessment that areas protected from human use are still inadequate, but the momentum for national parks and designated areas of special scientific interest is growing. Pinker feels that modern humans are not vile despoilers and plunderers who need to undo the Industrial Revolution, renounce technology and return to an ascetic harmony with nature. He prefers problem solving, in conjunction

*with demographic transition, densification and dematerialization
to reach Peak Children, Peak Farmland, Peak Timber, Peak Paper,
and Peak Car' (Pinker 2018).*

Even an enlightened environmentalist must face the alarming fact of the
effect of greenhouse gases on the earth's climate. Carbon monoxide, sulphur
dioxide, oxides of nitrogen, and particulate matter continue to be spewed
into the atmosphere, together with thirty-eight billion tonnes of carbon
dioxide and methane (the main greenhouse gases) every year, which, if left
unchecked, threaten to raise global temperatures by two to four degrees
Celsius. That will cause more heat waves, more floods, more droughts, lower
crop yields, species loss, melting of land ice with rising sea levels and diversion
of the Gulf Stream. The challenge is daunting. The sacrifice to bring carbon
emissions down to zero would require forgoing electricity, heating, cement,
steel, paper, travel, and affordable food and clothing. But preventing climate
change is a moral issue because it has potential to harm billions, particularly
the world's poor. The modern world must continue to decarbonise, further
develop carbon pricing, use the best renewable energy sources and perhaps
look again at nuclear energy. Pinker believes, with climate change, those who
know the most are the most frightened, but with nuclear power, those who
know the most are the least frightened. The benefits of advanced (Generation
IV) nuclear energy are valuable – people in the developing world could skip
the middle rungs (fossil fuel stages) of the energy ladder. Alldred, who was a
consultant to UK Nyrex in the late 1980s, still disagrees: 'the people proposing
a nuclear waste repository in Cumbria – their morality was zero; their
readiness to ignore science for corporate advancement was breath-taking;
and the conclusion I drew for my report was that the 250,000 year half-life
of nuclear wastes made them impossible to manage'. But claims exist that
the problems of nuclear waste do not come anywhere close to approaching
the problems of fossil fuel waste. The <u>World Nuclear Association</u> provides
a comparison of deaths due to accidents among different forms of energy
production. In their comparison, deaths per TWh/yr of electricity produced
(in the UK and USA) from 1970 to 1992 are quoted as 885 for hydropower,
342 for coal, 85 for natural gas, and 8 for nuclear.

David Bodansky originally set out the environmental paradox of nuclear
power in *Environmental Practice* back in 2001:

*Concern about nuclear waste disposal is probably even more
widespread than concern over reactor safety, perhaps because*

nuclear wastes are thought to threaten not only ourselves but also future generations. For the United States, the relevant nuclear waste is primarily the 'spent fuel' that is removed from a reactor at the end of the fuel's useful life. The volume of spent fuel is very small. It is in solid form, contained in many individual thin-walled protective metal cylinders. For disposal, these cylinders are to be placed in rugged thick-walled canisters and deposited in tunnels that are deep in an underground repository. Retrieval of the canisters and wastes is to be possible for the first 100 years or so, and then the repository is to be sealed.

The U.S. waste disposal program is now focused on the study of a potential repository at Yucca Mountain, Nevada. If a decision is made by the federal government to proceed with Yucca Mountain, the decision will undoubtedly face vigorous political and legal challenges.

The goal in designing the repository is to keep appreciable amounts of radioactive materials from reaching the biosphere. Basic factors working to make this possible include the small volume of the wastes, the decrease with time in the level of radioactivity, the dry environment at Yucca Mountain, the corrosion resistance of the metal canisters, which hold the wastes, and the slow rate at which water moves to and from the repository region.

Nuclear wastes and carbon dioxide are closely linked, because a direct way to reduce carbon dioxide emissions is to use nuclear fuel instead of coal to generate electricity. This is exemplified by France, which obtains about 75% of its electricity from nuclear power. The carbon dioxide emissions per capita for France in 1999 were 66%, those of Germany 87%, and of those for Italy 71%. Comparisons normalized to gross domestic product show an even greater advantage for France. If the United States had entirely replaced coal plants by nuclear plants for electricity generation, the 1998 carbon dioxide emissions would have been 32% lower. More extensive electrification of the energy economy could provide further gains.

The problems created by carbon dioxide are much greater than those created by nuclear wastes in terms of the numbers of people impacted, the severity of the impacts, and the immediacy of the dangers. Unfortunately, society does not yet appear ready to accept the minute risks from the one to help forestall the tremendous risks from the other (Bodansky, 2001).

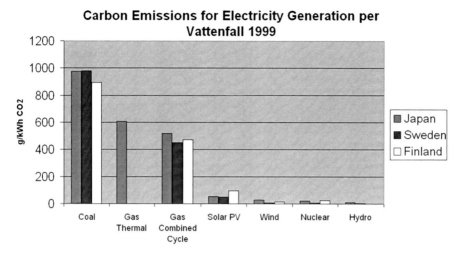

Immediately we run into many issues. The cynical view of long-term disposal in the UK is that the NIMBY tendency means that the aim is to prove that West Cumbria is the place to put it, as that is the only area likely not to kick up too much of a stink. Everything has its downsides. It is all about balancing the benefits and dis-benefits as best as possible. Roll on nuclear fusion, but only if humanity can grapple with balanced limits to our energy usage during the Anthropocene as clearly outlined by Mike Berners-Lee in his book *There Is No Planet B.* (Berners-Lee, 2019).

Greenhouse gases
Klein, in *This Changes Everything,* also emphasises that the clock is ticking as regards climate change. The externalities are staggering. Not only do fossil fuel companies receive $775 billion to $1 trillion in annual global subsidies, but also they pay nothing for the privilege of treating our shared atmosphere as a free waste dump – the greatest market failure the world has ever seen (Best et al, 2012; Stern, 2006). Deregulated capitalism and unrestrained market forces were exactly the race to the bottom that so many warned they would be. It is Kevin Anderson of the Tyndall Centre for Climate Change Research, one of Britain's top climate experts, who has most forcefully built the case that our grow-based economic logic is now in fundamental conflict with atmospheric limits. Wealthy countries need to start cutting their greenhouse gas emissions by something like eight to ten per cent a year – and they need to start right now (Klein, 2014).

Methods of capturing and storing carbon dioxide will also be critical because the 'greenhouse' needs actual dismantling to prevent global temperature rise. We need to recruit carbon-hungry plants, build with wood, convert biomass to charcoal, scrub CO_2 from smokestacks, and develop bioenergy with carbon capture and storage. Climate engineering or geoengineering may also have to be considered, but then whose hand would be on the world's thermostat (Pinker, 2018)? Klein fears a future of climate-change-fuelled disaster capitalism – profiteering disguised as emission reduction, privatised hyper-militarised borders and, quite possibly, high-risk geoengineering when things spiral out of control (Klein, 2014).

Not surprisingly, Kingsnorth also takes this different view from Pinker. He condemns the corporate spivs (whom he also calls neo-environmentalists). He feels the green movement has plunged into a full-on midlife crisis:

> 'Unable to significantly change the system or public behaviour assailed by a rising movement of 'sceptics' and by public boredom with being hectored about carbon and consumption, the movement has been colonised by a new breed of corporate spivs for whom sustainability is just another opportunity for selling things; the old greens are seeing a nasty realisation dawn: despite all their work, their passion, their commitment and the aforementioned fact that most of what they have been saying has been broadly right – they are losing' (Kingsnorth, 2017).

Now, neo-environmentalists are attempting to break through the lines of an old orthodoxy that is visibly exhausted and confused. They affirm that nature is more resilient than fragile. Wilderness does not exist; all of it has been influenced by humans at some time. Humans like development, and you can't stop them having it. Nature is tough and will adapt to this. Neo-environmentalists are distinguished by their attitude to new technologies, which they almost see as uniformly positive, for example, biotechnology, synthetic biology, geothermal energy (from supercritical heated water and 'natural nuclear' from beneath the earth's crust) and perhaps the aforementioned geoengineering.

The Oxford Geoengineering Programme (www.geoengineering.ox.ac.uk) defines geoengineering as deliberate large-scale intervention in the earth's natural systems to counteract climate change. It is a contentious subject and rightly so. Solar Radiation Management techniques aim to reflect a small proportion of the Sun's energy back into space, counteracting the temperature rise caused by increased levels of greenhouse gases in the atmosphere, which absorb energy and raise temperatures. Some proposed SRM techniques include: increasing the reflectiveness of clouds or the land surface so that more of the Sun's heat is reflected back into space (**albedo enhancement**), or introducing small, reflective particles into the upper atmosphere to reflect some sunlight before it reaches the surface of the earth (**stratospheric aerosols**).

Carbon Dioxide Removal techniques aim to remove carbon dioxide from the atmosphere, directly countering the increased greenhouse effect and ocean acidification. These techniques would have to be implemented on a global scale to have a significant impact on carbon dioxide levels in the atmosphere. Some proposed CDR techniques include:

- **Afforestation**. Engaging in a global-scale tree planting effort.
- **Biochar**. 'Charring' biomass and burying it so that its carbon is locked up in the soil.
- **Bio-energy with Carbon Capture and Sequestration**. Growing biomass, burning it to create energy and capturing and sequestering the carbon dioxide created in the process.
- **Ambient Air Capture**. Building large machines that can remove carbon dioxide directly from ambient air and store it elsewhere.
- **Ocean Fertilisation**. Adding nutrients to the ocean in selected locations to increase primary production, which draws down carbon dioxide from the atmosphere.
- **Enhanced Weathering**. Exposing large quantities of minerals that will react with carbon dioxide in the atmosphere and storing the resulting compound in the ocean or soil.
- **Ocean Alkalinity Enhancement**. Grinding up, dispersing, and dissolving rocks such as limestone, silicates, or calcium hydroxide in the ocean to increase its ability to store carbon and directly ameliorate ocean acidification. (www.geoengineering.ox.ac.uk, 2018).

Peter Beaumont, a senior reporter on *The Guardian's* Global Development desk, writes in the newspaper that all this sounds like the stuff of science fiction: the creation, using balloons or jets, of a man-made atmospheric sunshade to shield the most vulnerable countries in the Global South against the worst effects of global warming. But scientists, from countries including Bangladesh, Brazil, China, Ethiopia, India, Jamaica and Thailand, have joined the debate, arguing in the journal *Nature* that poor countries should take a lead in the field since they have most to gain or lose from the technology. In an interview with Reuters, Dr Atiq Rahman, Director of the Bangladesh Centre for Advanced Studies and the article's lead author, amplified his arguments:

'Clearly [solar radiation management geoengineering] could be dangerous, but we need to know whether, for countries like Bangladesh, it would be more or less risky than passing the 1.5C warming goal. This matters greatly to people from developing countries and our voices need to be heard.'

'The overall idea [of solar geoengineering] is pretty crazy, but it is gradually taking root in the world of research', said Rahman. (Beaumont, 2018).

The Oxford Geoengineering Programme admits we do not know for certain what level of greenhouse gases in the atmosphere is compatible with a stable climate and healthy oceans, but many scientists believe that stabilising at 450 parts per million volume of carbon dioxide (eqv) would give us a 50:50 probability of limiting increases in global mean temperature below two degrees Celsius, the threshold for 'dangerous' climate change.

So, there are two uncertainties:

- *The level at which we will manage to stabilise greenhouse gases.* This is a function of political will and technical ability.
- *The responsiveness of the climate system to increased greenhouse gas levels.* We may be lucky and have a small climate response to a large change in greenhouse gases. Or we may be unlucky and have a large climate response to a small change in greenhouse gases. No one knows for sure.

If humans continue on the current emissions path and are unlucky and the climate response is large, amplified by feedbacks, or the ability of human and natural systems to adapt is insufficient, the consequences could be dire for people and the planet. It is possible that by deploying geoengineering we may be able to forestall these consequences and to protect critically vulnerable natural ecosystems, such as the arctic or coral reefs, from damage that otherwise could no longer be avoided.

Given the uncertainties and stakes involved, it is important that we conduct research to determine if any of the proposed geoengineering techniques could be employed without creating countervailing side effects. It is far from certain that any of them could be. (www.geoengineering.ox.ac.uk, 2018). And it is notable that none of the projects from Intellectual Ventures mentioned in *SuperFreakonomics*, by Steven Levitt and Stephen Dubner in 2009, have so far been taken forward. As yet, there is no sign of 'a garden hose to the sky', 'a chimney to the sky', or soggy mirrors and water vapour boats. So it would be extremely unwise to rely on geoengineering as a 'silver bullet' for climate change. Instead humanity should concentrate on limiting methane and CO_2 production.

Caterpillars and butterflies

The traditional green focus on 'limits' is dismissed as naïve by neo-environmentalists who tend to exhibit an excitable enthusiasm for markets. Tied in with this is an almost religious attitude to the scientific method. This is all presented as 'pragmatism' but is actually something rather different: an attempt to exclude from the green debate any interventions based on morality, emotion, intuition, spiritual connection or simple human feeling.

Kingsnorth feels the neo-environmentalists are at least half right. They are right to say that the human-scale, convivial approaches of those 1970s thinkers are never going to work if the world continues to formulate itself according to the demands of late-capitalist industrialism. They are right to say that a world of nine billion people, all seeking the status of middle-class consumers, cannot be sustained by vernacular approaches. They are right to say that the human impact on the planet is enormous and irreversible. They are right to say that traditional conservation efforts sometimes idealised a pre-industrial culture. And they are right to say that greens have hit a wall, and that continuing to ram their heads against it is not going to knock it down. But no one ever suggested there was any such thing as 'pristine pre-human nature' – conservationists just believed there were still large-scale, functioning ecosystems worth protecting. For example, the Amazon is not important because it is 'untouched'; it's important because it is wild, in the sense that it is self-willed. It is lived in and from by humans, but it is not created or controlled by them. No species dominates the mix. It is a complex, working eco-system that is also a human-culture system, because in any worthwhile world the two are linked. Nature has a practical, cultural, emotional and even spiritual value, which is necessary for our well-being. The neo-environmentalists have no time for this kind of fluff. The wild is dead, and what remains of nature is for people. It is an anti-scientific belief that non-human life has any value beyond what we very modern humans can make use of (Kingsnorth, 2014).

Berry is, of course, passionate in this area. The defenders of nature and wilderness – like their enemies, the defenders of the industrial economy – sometimes sound as if the natural and the human were two separate estates. But these pure categories do not exist. Pure nature, anyhow, is not good for humans to live in, and humans do not want to live in it – or not for very long. Humans desire basic amenities: clothing, shelter, cooked food, the company of friends. It is equally true that a condition that is *purely* human is not good for people to live in, and people do not want to live there for very long either. The people who want clean air, clean streams and wild forests are the people who no longer have them. People cannot live apart from nature, and yet people cannot live in nature without changing it. This is true of all creatures. But unlike other creatures, humans must make a choice as to the kind and scale of the difference they make.

Nature, then, is not only our source but also our limit and measure. Nature and human culture – wildness and domesticity – are not opposed but are interdependent. If the human economy is to be fitted into the natural economy in such a way that both may thrive, the human economy must be built to proper scale. The scale of agriculture, from an economic point of view, is too big, but from a demographic point of view, the scale is too small. When there are enough people on the land to use it but not enough to husband it, the soil fertility diminishes and the soil itself disappears in water and wind erosion.

The survival of wilderness – of places that we do not change, where we allow the existence even of creatures we perceive as dangerous – is necessary. Whether we go to those places or not, we need to know they exist. We need great public wildernesses, and millions of small private ones too – on every farm and city lot. We must not go to wildernesses to escape the ugliness and the dangers of the present human economy. The wild and the domestic must have continuity between them. When the human estate becomes so precarious, our only recourse is to move it back toward the estate of nature. We undoubtedly need better plant and animal species than nature provided us. But we are beginning to see that they can be **too** much better, too dependent on us and on 'the economy', and too expensive. We do not need species that will not produce at all without expensive fertilisers and chemicals. One of the strangest characteristics of the industrial economy is the ability to increase production again and again without ever noticing – or without acknowledging – the *costs* of production. Can we afford a bushel of grain at the cost of five to twenty bushels of topsoil lost to erosion (Berry, 2017)? However, it would not be out of order to remind Berry that not everyone has access to the agricultural resources of Kentucky. Singapore or Hong Kong could not entertain these rural idylls that some might long for, and asking people in the Kalahari Desert to affect a relationship with the land, other than one of wresting basic sustenance from it, is well-nigh impossible (Alldred, personal communication, 2018).

To make some continuity between nature and humans, we have only two sources of instruction: nature herself and our cultural traditions. Listening to apologists for the industrial economy, we get the idea that it is somehow our goodness (trying to feed the hungry) that makes so much destruction. Respect for nature causes us to doubt this, and our cultural tradition confirms and illuminates our doubt: no good thing is destroyed by goodness; good things are destroyed by wickedness. Since the start of the industrial revolution, there have been voices urging that this inheritance may be safely replaced by intelligence, information, energy and money. No idea could be more dangerous (Berry, 2017)!

Economics is not a matter of discovering laws or curves: it is essentially a question of design, choices and incentives. It is time to change the cradle-to-grave manufacturing supply chain of take, make, use, and lose. Enriching for some this may be, but it runs counter to the living world, which recycles life's building blocks. Quotas, tiered pricing and environmental taxes can have a significant effect – the more you use, the more you pay. In practice, they fall short because they are rarely set at the level required and their introduction is delayed by governments fearing loss of competitiveness or corporate backing. What is needed instead is a paradigm of regenerative design.

Can we do business in the Doughnut?
Some options in the 'Corporate To-Do List' to move from the linear degenerative 'caterpillar' economy to a regenerative 'butterfly' economy:
   a) Do nothing – no longer a smart strategy
   b) Do what pays – 'green branding' to boost company profits – still a long way off what is needed
   c) Do our fair share – in switching to sustainability, but it almost never adds up
   d) Do no harm – designing products and businesses that aim for zero environmental impact
   e) Be generous – give back to the living systems, for example, in the carbon cycle, the phosphorus cycle, the nitrogen cycle and the water cycle.

What can we learn from nature's 3.8 billion years of experimentation, and what are the design features that enable a regenerative 'industrial butterfly' to take flight? The circular butterfly economy runs on renewable energy. The leftovers from one production process become the source materials for the next. Its two nutrient cycles are *biological* nutrients (soil, plants and animals) and *technical* nutrients (plastics, synthetics and metals). Biological nutrients should be harvested no faster than nature regenerates them. Technical nutrients must be designed to be restored – through repair, reuse, refurbishment and recycling.

Some examples are: rooftops that grow food, gather the Sun's energy and welcome wildlife; pavements that absorb storm water then release it into aquifers; buildings that sequester carbon dioxide, clean the air, treat their own wastewater and turn sewage back into rich soil nutrients; renewable energy microgrids that would turn every household into an energy provider; and dedicated public transport routes that would make the cheapest form of travel the fastest.

Today's majority ubiquitous business mind-set is focused on creating just one form of value – financial – for shareholders. Instead the question should be, 'How many diverse benefits can we layer into this?' But to date circular economy strategies have typically been top-down, in-house, opaque and fragmented. Regenerative industrial design can only be fully realised if it is underpinned by regenerative economic design. This calls for rebalancing the roles of the market, the commons and the state. This redesign process will emerge from innovative experiments.

The Open Source Circular Economy movement is a worldwide network of innovators who aim to create the knowledge commons to unleash the full potential of circular manufacturing outside as well as inside factory walls. Transparency is the key. Every day, the open-source knowledge commons grows and becomes more useful (e.g. www.asknature.org).

The business of business should be to contribute to a thriving world. The growing family of enterprise structures that are distributive by design can be regenerative by design too. Regenerative enterprise needs the support of financial partners seeking to invest long-term. Finance should support the whole economy by turning savings and credit into productive investments that deliver long-term social and environmental value. So the global financial system needs to shrink, simplify, diversify and deleverage – separating customers' deposit accounts from speculation; regulation against becoming too big, too leveraged, and too complex; and a global financial transactions tax to rein in high frequency trading. State-led development banks, pension funds and credit unions should offer 'patient capital' for renewable energy technologies and public transport systems.

Meeting science-based targets will mean forcing some of the most profitable companies on the planet to forfeit trillions of dollars of future earnings by leaving the vast majority of proven fossil fuel reserves in the ground, often in some of the poorest parts of the world (Fullerton, 2011). Because trading in pollution has many problems. The scheme of international carbon trading modelled on the cap-and-trade system is deeply flawed. The problem is that even the very best green projects are being made ineffective as climate responses because for every tonne of carbon dioxide the developers keep out of the atmosphere, a corporation in the industrialised world is able to pump a ton into the air, using offsets to claim the pollution has been neutralised. The EU's Emissions Trading System has not reduced greenhouse gas emissions. The worst polluters have had little to no obligation to cut emissions at source; indeed, the offset projects have resulted in an *increase* in emissions worldwide. (Corporate European Observatory, Life Beyong Emissions Trading, 2014). Rather than getting the polluters to pay for the mess they have created – a basic principle of environmental justice – taxpayers and ratepayers have heaped cash on them, and for a scheme that hasn't even worked (Klein, 2014).

Better to invest in real renewable energy alternatives – solar panels and wind power. A study from the Canadian Centre for Policy Alternatives, in 2012, compared the public value from a $5 billion oil pipeline and the value that could be derived from investing the same amount in green economic alternatives. If $5 billion is spent on public transit, building retrofits, and renewable energy, economies can gain three times as many jobs in the short term, while simultaneously helping to reduce the chances of catastrophic warming in the long term (Klein, 2014).

The state and decentralised ownership are key to promoting regenerative economic design by restructuring taxes and regulations, being a transformative investor and empowering the dynamism of the commons in renewable energy. Industry's focus should be moved away from raising *labour* productivity and towards raising *resource* productivity – this typically generates more jobs. The decentralised ownership model has the benefit of pushing against the trend toward utterly unsustainable wealth inequality – the ability to create wealth is gradually dispersed to the workers themselves and to the communities sustained by the presence of well-paying jobs (Klein, 2014).

Ecological footprints
Jim Kitchen, ex-director of the Sustainable Development Commission, is an advocate of ecological footprints. The ecological footprint is defined as the biologically productive area needed to provide for everything people use: fruits and vegetables, fish, wood, fibres, absorption of carbon dioxide from fossil fuel use, and space for buildings and roads. Footprints and biocapacity can be

compared at the individual, regional, national or global scale. Both footprints and biocapacity change every year with the number of people, per person consumption, efficiency of production, and productivity of ecosystems. At a global scale, footprint assessments show how big humanity's demand is compared to what planet Earth can renew.

'The average world citizen has an eco-footprint of about 2.7 global average hectares while there are only 2.1 global hectares of bioproductive land and water per capita on Earth. This means that humanity has already overshot global biocapacity by thirty per cent and now lives unsustainably by depleting stocks of "natural capital". 'Humanity's ecological footprint was 7.0 billion gha in 1961 and increased to 20.6 billion gha in 2014. Because of agricultural intensification, biocapacity was at 9.6 billion gha in 1961 and grew to 12.2 billion gha in 2014.' (Wikipedia, 2014).

The UK's average ecological footprint is 5.45 global hectares per capita (gha with variations between regions ranging from 4.80 gha (Wales) to 5.56 gha (East England). The average per country ranges from over 10 to under 1 global hectare per person. There is also a high variation within countries, based on individual lifestyle and economic possibilities (Wikipedia, 2018).

The monopoly of monetary metrics is over: it's time for a panoply of living metrics. Real-time measurements of a city's water use, carbon emissions, electricity use and river health could be recorded, and dynamic trends monitored year on year, to map global material footprints.

Human Welfare and Ecological Footprints compared

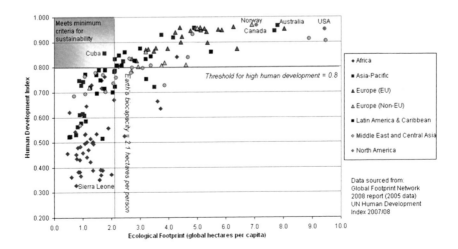

Living metrics for business are offered by the MultiCapital Scorecard through a matrix of performance indicators to score their sustainability. This enables governments to proactively support regenerative enterprises. The next leap for such business metrics is to go beyond do-no-harm sustainability towards rewarding generous design.

A circular economy with regenerative distributive design will head towards the Doughnut's safe and just space. But what is the future for GDP (Raworth, 2017)? We will return to this question in Chapter 9, but first we should consider reason and its limits.

Two minds

For centuries, alchemy (the creation of 'gold') has been the basis of our system of money and banking and the quest for growth. Governments pretended that paper money could be turned into gold even when there was more of the former than the latter. Banks pretended that short-term riskless deposits could be used to finance long-term risky investments to provide growth. In both cases, the alchemy is the apparent transformation of risk into safety. In recent times, banks have been financing themselves with too little equity and holding too few liquid assets (King, 2016).

Since 2008, regulators have been tightening up on the freedoms of banks. Moreover, the market itself has imposed its own discipline on banks. Banks have become smaller and many turned themselves back into more traditional commercial banks. Individuals obviously still need this traditional banking (King, 2016). The mantra 'only spend what you have, not what the bank will give you' has one exception, which is a responsible 'budgeted debt' – that is, buying something we need now but cannot afford now. The obvious example is a mortgage to buy a house and so have somewhere to live. This is clearly an example of 'buy now, pay later', but it is wise to ensure that the value of the house could cover the debt if it were sold. Still radical uncertainty can trap the unfortunate in 'negative equity' so in general it is worth saying that loans for non-essential items are a bad idea (Beynon, 2011).

Since the 2008 bank bailouts were so huge, it is surprising that more has not been done. Banks should continue to separate into (a) safe and liquid 'narrow' banks, carrying out payment services and (b) risky and illiquid 'wide' banks, performing all other activities.

King feels it is time to replace the lender of last resort (LOLR) with the pawnbroker for all seasons (PFAS). The aim is threefold: firstly, to ensure that all deposits are backed by actual cash or a guaranteed contingent claim on reserves at the central bank; secondly, to ensure that the provision of liquidity insurance is mandatory and paid upfront; and thirdly, to design a system which in effect imposes a tax on the degree of alchemy. Such a reform programme will take decades (King, 2016).

This is quite a rational and scientific approach from Mervyn King. But Wendell Berry, being an American agrarian conservationist, believes that modern human beings are involved in a kind of 'lost-ness', in which most people are participating more or less unconsciously in the destruction of the natural world and therefore the source of their own lives. Obviously we need to use our intelligence and reason to understand the issues of the natural world. But how much intelligence have we got? And what sort of intelligence is it that we have? And how, at its best, does human intelligence work? He supposes there are two kinds of human mind: the Rational Mind and the Sympathetic Mind.

The Rational Mind, without being anywhere perfectly embodied, is the mind all of us are supposed to be trying to have. Our schools exist mainly to educate, propagate and authorise the Rational Mind – objective, analytical and empirical; considering facts, truth by experimentation, and uncorrupted by preconception. It is the official mind of science, industry, banking and government. It is the mind of the Enlightenment.

The Sympathetic Mind differs from the Rational Mind, not by being unreasonable, but by refusing to make reason the servant of things it considers precedent and higher. It is under the influence of certain inborn, fundamental likes and dislikes. It is moved by affection for its home place, the local topography, the local memories and the local creatures. It is the mind of The Bible (Matthew 18:12–13).

'Let us see how the two kinds of mind would deal with the dilemma of the lost sheep.

The rationalist has a hundred sheep because he has a plan for that many. The one who has gone astray has escaped not only from the flock but also from the plan. That this particular sheep should stray off in this particular place at this particular time, though it is perfectly in keeping with the nature of sheep and the nature of the world, is not at all in keeping with a rational plan. What is to be done? Well, it certainly would NOT be rational to leave the ninety-nine, exposed, as they would be to the further whims of nature, in order to search for the one. Wouldn't it be best to consider the lost sheep a 'trade-off' for the safety of the ninety-nine? Having thus agreed to his loss, the doctrinaire rationalist would then work *his way through a series of reasonable questions. What would be an acceptable risk? What would be an acceptable loss? Would it not be good to do some experiments to determine how often sheep may be expected to get lost? If one sheep is likely to get lost every so often, then would it not be better to have perhaps 110 sheep? Or should one insure the flock against such expectable losses? The annual insurance premium would equal the market value of how many sheep? What is likely to be the cost of the labour of looking for one lost sheep after quitting time? How much time spent looking would equal the market value of the lost sheep? Should one not consider splicing a few firefly genes into one's sheep DNA so that strayed sheep would glow in the dark? And so on…*

BUT the shepherd is a shepherd because he embodies the Sympathetic Mind. Because he is a man of sympathy, a man devoted to the care of sheep, a man who knows the nature of sheep and of the world, the shepherd of the parable is not surprised or baffled by his problem. He does not hang back to argue over risks, trade-offs, actuarial data, or market values. He does not quibble over fractions. He goes without hesitating to hunt for the lost sheep because he has committed himself to the care of the whole hundred, because he understands his work as the fulfilment of his whole trust, because he loves the sheep and because he knows or imagines what it is to be lost. He does what he does on behalf of the whole flock because he wants to preserve himself as a whole shepherd. He has a particular affection for that particular sheep. To the Rational Mind, all sheep are the same; they are interchangeable (like clones or machine parts or members of 'the work force'). To the Sympathetic Mind, each sheep is an individual whose value is never entirely reducible to market value.

If you want to hire somebody to take care of your hundred sheep, you had better look past the 'animal scientist' and hire the shepherd of the parable.' (Berry, 2016).

The Rational Mind is motivated by fear of being wrong. The Sympathetic Mind is motivated by fear of being unloving. The Rational Mind is exclusive; the Sympathetic Mind is inclusive. The Rational Mind is scornful of limits but the Sympathetic Mind is occupied precisely with the study of limits, both natural and human (Berry, 2016).

CHAPTER 9

ADDICTED TO THE ANTHROPOCENE

IT MAY BE NATURAL to think of man as the centre of the universe. The next seductive extension is to put ourselves at the centre of our own respective little 'bubble'. We need to retain the ability to break out of these bubbles. Bartlett (2018) notes that democracy theorists from Aristotle onwards have realised the importance of healthy and independent civil-led bodies – charities, conservation groups, sports teams and so on – that are neither business nor government. Alexis de Tocqueville (1835) wrote, in *Democracy in America*, that private associations are 'schools for democracy'. Autocrats and dictators always dismantle independent civil society. Chatting online without forming meaningful bonds is no match for the power of organised tech bureaucracies. There is much to fear from monopolies because of their concentration of power, data and control over the public space.

Big Tech

The great tech monopolies have prospered at the expense of journalism. The industry's decline is desperately worrying because almost every story that uncovers shadowy influences in our politics – lobbying, manipulation, and corruption – is the result of painstaking, expensive journalism. And perhaps the final stage is when economic power morphs into what Marxists sometimes call 'cultural hegemony': where domination can be achieved through controlling the ideas and assumptions available to the public. Over the years, the big tech firms have very carefully cultivated the Californian Ideology: a fusion of San Francisco bohemianism, entrepreneurial free market zeal and an anti-establishment pitch for social justice and equality. Total victory for the tech monopolies is not over economics or politics – it's over assumptions, ideas and possible futures. Because when that happens, Big Tech won't need to lobby or buy out competitors. They will have so insinuated themselves in our lives and minds that we won't be able to imagine a world without them (Bartlett, 2018).

Love of money

Meanwhile, King still finds it difficult to imagine a world without growth. Many of the problems that seem to overwhelm us – poverty, rising inequality, crumbling infrastructure, ethnic tensions within and between countries – could all be eased by rates of growth that before the 2008 crisis seemed quite normal. King sees that the troubled world economy is a result of the disequilibrium that led to the crisis itself (King, 2016). Beynon wants to counter an overly anthropocentric focus by emphasising what God does not say about man and money. God gives prosperity? Beware this 'prosperity gospel'. Riches are not a sign of God's blessing, and poverty is not a sign of his anger (and nor is disability or illness). God loves poverty? Beware this 'poverty gospel' also. God does not love poverty. Martin Luther is quoted as saying '…*if silver and gold are good creations of God, which we can use both for the needs of our neighbour and for the glory of God, is not a person silly… if he refrains from them as if they are evil'*.

Yet this is dangerous territory, because the love of money is so dangerous. People could easily excuse selfishness and indulgence. But the key point is to see that the answer does not lie in shunning money, but in using money rightly. Some will have grown up with money on hand and so presume they can buy what they like, when they like (and then get caught out when they can't afford it). Others will have counted every penny and naturally be cautious about spending (even when they have lots in the bank). It is important to have a good deal of self-awareness, honesty, and respect for other people doing things differently (Beynon, 2011).

The Archbishop of Canterbury, the Right Reverend Justin Welby, believes we are living in an ever more broken society. Many of the richest ten per cent actually do little work but rather live off their income-generating wealth (whether that is property rentals or stocks and shares, as the elite did back in the eighteenth and nineteenth centuries – the 'rentiers', as Piketty calls them). Politicians struggle to stand up to global corporations who can easily move jobs and finance around the planet if conditions and corporation tax are more to their liking. Coordination problems abound in a capitalist economy, and control of events and outcomes is difficult. If wage cuts don't restore employment, then why should interest rate cuts restore spending? The analysis of the 'liquidity trap', which has underpinned much recent analysis of the reasons for slow growth, is based on the model of the economics of 'stuff' rather than the economics of 'stuff happens'. Radical uncertainty ('stuff happens') means that many of the markets in which prices might move to produce an equilibrium simply cannot and do not exist. And, as noted above,

Hyman Minsky argued that long periods of stability would create excessive confidence in the future, leading to the underpricing of risk and overpricing of assets, a boom in spending and activity, and excessive accumulation of debt, ending in a financial crash which, because of high debt burdens, would lead to a deep recession (King, 2016). This sounds awfully familiar, particularly if you are a citizen of Ireland, Iceland, Portugal, Italy, Spain or Greece.

Many people confused stability with sustainability prior to 2008. If domestic spending in the economy is too high, at some point real interest rates will have to rise and the trade deficit come down. But financial markets were complacent about the growing disequilibrium and believed real interest rates would stay low for a long time. The level of spending continued at unsustainably high levels in the US and UK and at unsustainably low levels in Germany and China. And the imbalance between countries – large trade surpluses and deficits – grew. In the long term, policy in the US and UK needs to bring about a shift away from domestic spending and towards exports, to reduce the trade deficit, to lower the leverage on household and bank balance sheets and to raise the rate of national saving and investment (King, 2016). We can all fall into thinking God likes what we happen to do and then look down on the other ways of doing things. This is not easy to work out, because we are not great at working out our own attitudes and we can never fully know someone else's. So it is possible that someone else is spending or saving unwisely but equally it is possible that they aren't. We are able to see what they are spending: but almost always we can't tell why. Good advice, surely though, is to always try to balance the budget! And it is worth saying again that loans for non-essential items are a bad idea.

Some will need to spend money. All should be thoughtful about what to spend money on, but not make a virtue of not spending. Some will tend towards limitation without enjoyment and never spend; others will tend towards enjoyment without limitation, and make excuses for excessive spending. The seventeenth century Puritan believers spoke about 'moderation'.

Some will need to save money. Saving for planned expenditure is much better than borrowing and having to pay back interest. Some saving for emergencies means having some degree of 'buffer' that softens unexpected blows (radical uncertainty) and avoids having to go into debt. Saving for a pension is a way to avoid dependency in later life. Some savings can be passed on to dependents.

Not all of us will have much scope for saving, but some will. It can be a good and wise thing to do (Beynon, 2011). This is the complete opposite of allowing governments to accumulate huge national debts to be a millstone around the necks of future generations. These same governments are then totally reliant on economic growth to balance the books.

Growth agnostic

However, Kate Raworth's **seventh** and final idea is more radical. **Be agnostic about growth (GDP) – from growth addicted to growth agnostic.**

No country has ever ended human deprivation without a growing economy. Here is agreement with Mervyn King. And no country has ever ended ecological degradation with one. The reality bit! The goal is to get into the Doughnut by ending deprivation and degradation at the same time. We need to design an economy that promotes human prosperity whether GDP is going up, down or holding steady. Being agnostic in this way calls for the transformation of financial, political and social structures.

It is rare indeed to come across a graph plotting several centuries of past GDP growth, let alone a diagram suggesting what might happen in centuries ahead. Does the graph line start to flatten out or keep rising rapidly off the top of the page (exponential growth)? The first option is awkward, the second unconscionable. A great shortcoming of humans is our inability to understand exponential function.

Actually, early economists acknowledged what most of their successors have since ignored: that economic growth must eventually reach a limit – hence the S-curve of growth. If we humans can learn to safely navigate the Anthropocene without pushing our planet into a hostile state, the economies we create could keep on thriving – not growing, but thriving – for millennia.

Where are we now on the growth curve? Global economic growth is made up of around two hundred national economies with widely differing growth rates. Some low-income countries are at the take-off stage – can they leapfrog the wasteful and polluting technologies of the past and enter the Doughnut's safe and just space with distributive and regenerative designed economies? In many high-income countries sluggish GDP growth has been accompanied by widening income inequalities. It would take five planets, in terms of global ecological footprints, for everyone to live an Australian/Kuwaiti lifestyle. Many high-income countries are at the top of their S-curves. It is time to think about landing the economic plane, otherwise the promise of even slight GDP growth in the Western world will be secured only at the cost of accepting catastrophic climate damage.

The problems of diagnosing the disequilibrium in the build-up to the 2008 crisis were compounded by the fact that no single country on its own could easily have found a way to a new equilibrium in the absence of similar adjustments by other countries. So the real source of disagreement (keep on flying or prepare for landing) is more political than technical. The keep-on-flying passengers say that economic growth is a social and political necessity in every country. If growth wanes the risk of political instability rises and democracy would have to be abandoned. Instead technology optimists argue that fast-rising productivity of robots will drive a new wave of GDP growth. Green growth advocates argue for a decoupling, in that resource use (water, fertiliser, greenhouse gases) can fall, if (1) we rapidly shift energy supply into renewables; (2) we create a resource-efficient circular economy; and (3) we expand the 'weightless' economy made possible by digital products and services. The rate of decoupling would have to keep pace with GDP growth year on year.

The prepare-for-landing passengers believe it is too late for decoupling solutions. Economic growth is driven by labour, capital and by the increasing efficiency with which energy is converted into useful work. So the last two centuries of extraordinary growth in high-income countries is largely due to the availability of cheap fossil fuels. 'Landers' believe that GDP growth is likely to end within a few decades because renewable energy cannot be installed fast enough to meet demand. Landers believe it is time to go green without growth, adding that higher income inequalities do not make people happier anyway. However, our anthropocentric societies have evolved to expect growth and do not yet know how to live without it. If GDP growth is still needed but no longer possible, the political underpinnings of our world start to fall apart, with intense distributional conflicts re-emerging (Raworth, 2017).

Creation care

The Jubilee Community Benefit Society defines creation care as environmental and agricultural stewardship that incorporates flourishing, fairness, welfare and well-being (www.jubilee.coop). Tom McLeish, Professor of Physics at Durham University, believes that in even a brief survey of Old Testament literature, the various versions of the story of creation appear at almost every turn (as wisdom, prophecy and history). There is the ever-present tension of order and chaos. Wisdom of natural things takes time to acquire. In Robert Grosseteste, the Bishop of Lincoln (a thirteenth-century thinker), we see the desire to peer beneath the surface of phenomena, harnessing both keenness of observation and power of thought to reach an insight that only came to full flower eight centuries later (McLeish, 2014).

'Wisdom' in Proverbs is no abstract philosophical category: rather it is an intensely practical method of living most fruitfully in the real world

(Proverbs 8). Thinking about nature is not, in the Bible, a 'spare-time' activity: it is part of the healthy lives of individuals and communities, and part of the stories that carry them from their pasts towards their futures (Psalm 33). If the story of nature is intimately and irretrievably woven into the story of the people who live within it, then we can begin to see that physical and mental pain will inevitably be part of that relationship (Psalm 104). Jeremiah's message is simply that humankind and the physical world are so closely knit that replacing wisdom with foolishness (the abuse of nature) within this relationship can cause creation to unravel. The first quiet linking of creation and salvation that Isaiah 40 introduces as a single voice becomes a theme of much volume later in the Bible (McLeish, 2014).

There is creative tension between the chaotic and the ordered in nature, which lies within the foundation of science today. It is a narrative theme of human culture that is as old as any. It is depicted in the ancient biblical creation narratives, building through wisdom, poetic, and prophetic literature. McLeish feels the order and chaos are well represented by the comet, the storm and the earthquake. The Book of Job is one of the greatest nature writings of the ancient world. It calls to mind the creative task that asks nature the right questions at the right time: questions that open up paths of understanding rather than further confusion (McLeish, 2014).

Turning to the New Testament, the current created order holds an important place in the message of renewal that Paul sees as central to the Christian mission. It is in continuity with the Old Testament laws and prophets, but takes new immediacy and transformed life from the Easter events (Romans 8:18ff). The first Easter extends an invitation to participate in the coming into being of renewed creation. The gospel message extends the same beckoning finger that was extended to Job on his ash heap, offering an invitation to explore the possibilities of a 'new nature' (1 Corinthians 15:37). Without invoking the word 'wisdom' itself, Revelation has encoded the end of the search for wisdom. The dream seen at a distance from Psalms and Job becomes a reality. The perspective is no longer one of ignorance and fear (McLeish, 2014).

The cul-de-sacs of non-overlapping peaceful co-existence or parallel methodologies plague the conflict between science and theology, in the attempt to address nature/creation issues. But, as stated above, the deep impulse to understand the physical world is as old as any written record of human culture. McLeish feels that to better understand and interact with creation, instead of thinking in terms of theology **and** science, we should develop a theology **OF** science and a science **OF** theology. Every science discipline has its great questions that drive a direction from ignorance and puzzlement towards dawning understanding. The nature-wisdom tradition in the Bible is directional in the same sense. The special human aptitude for seeing into the natural world through scientific endeavour, like no other creature does, and finding an extraordinary resonance when we do, has been a strong theme of our theological story as well.

Crucially, humankind has moved from minor status in the biosphere to a dominant position. The human population now has critical influence over climate change, over fresh water provision and over crop cycles. This makes ignorance of the world (earthquakes and storms) even more frightening – for now we see that making the wrong move may alter radically the degree to which our planet is hospitable to human life. McLeish reminds us again that order and chaos are held in tension within creation, using the cell wall as an example. All the complexity of the lipid cell wall is 'controlled chaos' – removing the random molecular motion prevents its construction and is equivalent to reducing the temperature to absolute zero. No life operates there. We seem to hear resonances of the Lord's answer to Job. We might rail against the chaotic and complex elements of nature that threaten our well-being or escape our understanding, but when we respond to the invitation to peer into the beautiful structures of the natural world we are so interested in protecting, we see them built upon a microscopic world of disorder, which is the substrate of life itself. Science becomes, within a Christian theology, the grounded outworking of the 'ministry of reconciliation' between humankind and the world. Far from being a task that threatens to derail the narrative of salvation, it actually participates within it. A theology *of* science begins to circumvent the relentless contest over ground between theology *and* science (McLeish, 2014).

A theological perspective on science immediately recalibrates the proper length and pace of its story. Data suggesting that we are currently entering a period of very rapid climate change is beginning to reignite a healthy debate about our responsibilities to later generations, rather than simply ourselves. We need to recognise that long-term thinking and values will be under threat if that story goes quiet. The long biblical story of human responsibility to cherish the world, to recognise that we need to work with nature in knowledge and wisdom rather than ignorance, that the future does not lie in a return to some classical idyllic past but in transformation, and that there are questions that must be asked but that will go unanswered for a very long time; this constitutes a foundation for a healthy reappraisal of timescales. Nevertheless, a participatory and reconciliatory theology of science has a very practical consequence for individual worship and teaching within churches on these issues (McLeish, 2014).

We tell ourselves all kinds of similarly implausible 'no consequences' stories all the time – about how we can ravage the world and suffer no adverse effects. We extract and do not replenish and wonder why the fish have disappeared and the soil requires ever more 'inputs' (like phosphate) to stay fertile. We drive down wages, ship jobs overseas, destroy worker protections, and hollow out local economies. We offer sub-prime mortgages instead of steady jobs and then wonder why no one foresaw that a system built on bad debts would collapse.

Extractivism is a nonreciprocal, dominance-based relationship with the earth, one of purely taking. The last sixty years of 'extractive development' on the Pacific island of Nauru perfectly illustrates the consequences when extractivism supersedes stewardship: massive phosphate mining led to a scarred island interior and obscene riches, which led to obesity and a diabetes epidemic, followed by bad investment advice, Russian tax haven status, a huge shadow economy and eventually economic and ecological bankruptcy. Now, Nauru has had to resort to becoming an offshore refugee detention centre for the Australian government and it is gravely threatened by rising sea levels (Klein, 2014). Not many signs of harmony with nature or open borders there!

The economic airplane

King opens his final chapter with a quote from Georg Wilhelm Friedrich Hegel in *Lectures on the Philosophy of History* (1832). He states '*What experience and history teaches us is that people and governments have never learned anything from history, or acted on principles deduced from it*'. Without reform another crisis is certain. Extraordinarily low interest rates have fallen further and recovery has been anaemic (King, 2011). We must change course.

The economic airplane is heading for a destination that is degenerative and deeply divisive. So whether GDP goes up or down, it is time for high-income countries to create regenerative and distributive economies that engage the household, market, commons and state alike. Many sectoral transformations are needed – the contraction of old industries, less speculative finance and, instead, long-term investment in renewable energy, public transport and commons-based circular manufacturing. It calls for investing in sources of wealth from which all value flows, whether it is monetised or not.

We have an economy that needs to grow, whether or not it makes us thrive. We need an economy that makes us thrive, whether or not it grows. (Raworth, 2017).

Attempting to sustain GDP growth can drive governments to take desperate measures – they deregulate in an attempt to unleash new productive investment but instead unleash house price bubbles and debt crises; they 'cut red tape' but end up dismantling workers' rights. Better to admit it is time for the economic airplane to touch down (Raworth, 2017).

People can be healthy, solvent and literate and still not lead rich and meaningful lives. Fortunately, major dimensions of flourishing that are not captured by the standard metrics – the rights of women, children and minorities – are on a steady rise. But how do we reconcile the rat race of frenzied careerism, hollow consumption, mindless entertainment and lack of social morality? The philosopher Martha Nussbaum has laid out a set of 'fundamental capabilities' that all people should be given the opportunity to exercise (Nussbaum, 2000). After the expected – longevity, health, safety, literacy, knowledge, free expression and political participation – she would include aesthetic experience, recreation and play, enjoyment of nature, emotional attachments and the opportunities to reflect on and engage in one's own conception of a good life. Maslow revisited, perhaps.

Some pipe dreams have become a reality in the Western world at least: paid vacations, retirement, labour-saving devices, travel, connecting technologies, varied cuisine and more leisure time for recreational, intellectual and artistic creativity (Pinker, 2018). Unfortunately, across Western countries many of these dreams have been realised only on the back of huge public and private debt (excepting the top ten per cent of the income distribution who hold all the wealth in every country). Sovereign debt forgiveness, as advocated by Varoufakis, is necessary but not sufficient. Maintaining interest rates at very low levels for so long has raised asset prices and increased debt. Sovereign debts are likely to be a major headache for the world, both in emerging markets and in the euro area. For example, the inevitability of restructuring Greek debt means that the taxpayers of Germany and elsewhere will have to absorb substantial losses. Monetary union has created a conflict between a centralised elite on the one hand, and the forces of democracy at the national level on the other. This is extraordinarily dangerous. Seemingly Germany faces a terrible choice: German taxpayers take the hit or Germany calls a halt to the euro project. Of course, another more likely cause of the break-up of the euro area is that voters in the South will tire of the grinding and relentless burden of mass unemployment and the emigration of talented young people and instead put long-term benefits above the short-term costs of an exit (King, 2016).

Looking more globally, it is an obscenity that the previously colonised world, whose wealth has been plundered for 500 years, should be deemed to owe the 'rich' world money, and that this presumed debt should be so onerous that every year over $300 billion is transferred to the banks and financial institutions of the 'rich' nations. These debt repayments are not available to feed the hungry, to house the poor, or to provide healthcare, education, clean water, transport and pensions for people who have none of these amenities. Perhaps it would indeed be a blessing in disguise if the European Union and other Western trading blocs were to reform or disappear.

Matt Williams comes to more or less the same conclusions in 'Blessed are the poor?':

> *Perhaps it is time again to take a hard look at poverty, a word too often synonymous with 'Africa'. Many of us live and work in situations where we witness various levels of poverty or pain; nobody is pretending that Africa, or Malawi in particular, has a monopoly on suffering or extreme poverty. But there is a particularly acute challenge in seeing how little Malawians eat, or how few have access to decent medical care, or how many fail to get enough education to gain employment.*
>
> *One way to respond is simply acknowledging that resources should be spread more evenly, and we need to give from our excess to those who have less. However, we must also consider three other aspects here: –*
>
> 1. *Beware the materialistic trap of seeing humans only as financially constituted or as machines that run on pure money. To cut a long and often depressing story short, such an approach to foreign aid has consistently failed sub-Saharan Africa. People are inevitably involved in complex domestic and social relationships and power struggles that shape their lives. We make naïve assumptions, which miss this. Africa is no different in this respect from anywhere else, and merely throwing money at problems denies a proper biblical understanding of humanity.*
> 2. *The second problem, which an exclusive focus on 'redistribution' misses, is that Africans are by no means passive. Treating poverty as an emergency to which we constantly rush with sticky plasters perpetuates the assumption that the poor are basically useless. Yet visitors to*

Malawi will be struck by the courage and resourcefulness in the face of constant physical, economic, social, political and (fundamentally) spiritual adversity.

3. *Seeing the problem purely as 'they have less, we have more' turns into a mathematical issue just looking for a logical solution. But we need to step back and ask ourselves why such inequality exists and uncomfortable as it may be, whether we are at all responsible. Most people today acknowledge that we are part of a global village but the fact that people from every language and nation can meet on a level playing field such as Facebook hides massive power imbalances. The history of empires has led to trade arrangements extremely beneficial to the Western world but far less beneficial to the poor world. Try ordering a new iPhone in most of Central Africa! Malawi produces commodities like sugar and tea for which our companies pay as little as possible while thousands of labourers work for less than £1 per day.*

On a bigger scale, our Western lifestyle involves producing massive amounts of carbon dioxide, and simultaneously cutting down the trees that should be absorbing it. Taking the global situation seriously is simply part of the core Christian mandate to love one another. For some, 'justification by faith' comes to mean 'what we say about Christ is more important than what we do'. But Paul, for one, never allows us to think this way (for example Romans 15:25–28, 2 Corinthians 8–9, Galatians 2:10, Philippians 4:14–16).

So how do we respond to inequality and a lack of social justice that can feel overwhelming? Well, we must be constantly rooted in grace, remembering that otherwise (on our own) we are all in spiritual poverty. The Cross is about forgiveness and repentance so we must not refuse to be lovingly connected to fellow believers in Malawi. Paul arranged for support to be sent across vast distances of the Roman Empire, so likewise we must engage in picking up the baton from small-scale charities – the likes of The Raven Trust (if it is indeed to close in 2018 – www.theraventrust.org). At the other end of the spectrum, much has to change internationally – on the world money markets, IMF and the World Bank. Is a world parliament or a reformed United Nations the answer? Much prayer is needed here (Williams, 2017).

Social justice

Meanwhile, governments need to plan safe landings and become thriving, growth-agnostic economies. Politics, social structures and values need to change in high-income countries. There are, of course, no easy answers. It will take decades of experimentation and experience to come up with smart solutions.

What is the rate of return? The search for gain lodges dependency in continual GDP growth deep within the financial system. Money accumulates forever, thanks to interest, and is so underinvested in creating productive assets, from renewable energy systems to circular manufacturing. A currency bearing demurrage (a small fee incurred for holding money) is needed to encourage investment in regenerative enterprises in the financial future. The search for gain would be replaced by the search to maintain value. This idea is not far removed from negative interest rates, but it raises many challenging questions and implications for inflation and exchange rates, for capital flows and pension funds, etc. This is addressed by Monbiot in one of his ideas for a new world order, namely an International Clearing Union (Monbiot, 2003).

In the mid-twentieth century, growth shifted from being a policy option to a political necessity because of:

a) Hope for raising revenue without raising taxes
b) Fear of unemployment
c) Power of the G20 'family photo'.

To overcome this political addiction: firstly, build consensus for a higher-tax, higher-return public sector (tax justice and public investment underpin collective well-being). Secondly, end the injustice of tax loopholes, offshore havens, profit shifting, etc. Thirdly, shift both personal and corporate taxation away from taxing income streams and towards taxing accumulated wealth. Fourthly, shorten the standard paid working week to tackle unemployment and overwork. Fifthly, introduce some new metrics and rank countries in the G20 in terms of human health and education, along with income per person, instead of GDP.

We are socially locked into GDP growth through consumerism and inequality, which are rooted in the need for something to aspire to. Despite being far richer than kings of old, everyone is racing to 'keep up with the Joneses'. Reversing consumerism's financial and cultural dominance is set to be one of the twenty-first century's most gripping psychological dramas. Growth is a substitute for equality of income, but is it the best aspiration on offer? The New Economics Foundation suggests five simple acts to promote well-being and the art of living (Coote, 2010).

a) Connecting with people
b) Being active
c) Taking notice of the living world (see Paul Kingsnorth and Wendell Berry)
d) Learning new skills
e) Giving to others (see Graham Beynon)

Economists need to enable nations coming to the end of their GDP growth to learn to thrive without it.

Crypto-anarchy
Bartlett identifies one further area that threatens us all in the modern world – the spectre of crypto-anarchy. Computer technology is on the verge of providing the ability for individuals and groups to communicate and interact with each other in a totally anonymous manner. These developments, via encryption, will alter completely the nature of government regulation, the ability to tax and control economic interactions, the ability to keep information secret, and will even alter the nature of trust and reputation. It takes far more computing power to decrypt something than to encrypt it. The most popular crypto-anarchy technology at the moment is bitcoin. Transactions are collected into blocks and ordered chronologically into a block chain. Block chains also allow complicated computer code to be stored. A block chain social media platform would be untouchable – no government would be able to edit or remove hate speech, illegal images or terror propaganda. The reason this is so important is because future technology will increase further the ability of small groups of individuals to do great harm, which means the authorities will need greater power, not less. There will be much vulnerability because the security standards for the 'Internet of Things' devices are notoriously bad. Every day it gets a little simpler to be a cybercriminal.

And, of course, the challenge to government posed by bitcoin is potentially existential, because it is a direct challenge to the state monopoly over money. If money becomes independent, governments will struggle to pay for themselves. Just as there should be no taxation without representation, so there can be no representation without taxation, because there would be no money to provide services (Bartlett, 2018).

The Other half of *Oikos*

Kite surfing is a good metaphor for the future of GDP, with the value of products and services sold each year bobbing and dipping in response to the constantly evolving economy. As before, humanity's glass can easily look half empty (Kingsnorth, 2017). You can quickly find yourself turning to the economics of collapse and survival, which could help to make those very outcomes self-fulfilling. But ours is the first generation to understand about planetary damage and the last generation able to do something about it. The other concept contained within *oikos* is the stewardship of our planetary home. The polluter should pay. A 2011 survey by the UN Department of Economic and Social Affairs looked at how much it would cost for humanity to 'overcome poverty, increase food production to overcome hunger without degrading land and water resources, and avert the climate change catastrophe'. The price tag was $1.9 trillion for the next forty years, investing especially in developing countries (UN Dept of ESA, 20110. (The only rational way forward is to fully embrace the principle already well established in Western law: the polluter pays. The top five oil companies were pulling in $900 billion in profits from 2001 to 2010 (Weiss, 2011). And what about 'climate debt'? The failed Yasuni plan for developed countries to pay for Ecuadorian rainforest not to be cut down, and to use those funds for renewable energy transition, was based on the premise that Ecuador, like all developing countries, is owed a debt for the inherent injustice of climate change caused by the Global North, accrued over two centuries. (Wallace, 2013; Klein, 2014).

We have the technology, know-how and financial means to address climate breakdown and to end extreme poverty. This makes the political process of adjudicating between alternative policies as important as ever, if we are to break free from our anthropocentric addiction (Raworth, 2017). So finally it is time to draw together some possible solutions – this is the challenge of the final chapter.

CHAPTER 10

TOWARDS A REVALUED
STANDARD OF LIVING

WHERE CAN WE SEARCH out the ideas that can be turned into alternative policies to address the two existential threats of inequality and ecological damage? It seems a reasonable approach to distil together the best ideas from authors who actually acknowledge and believe in the existence of the inequality issues and climate change/ecological issues that need addressing. Then we can start the journey to a revalued standard of living.

On the inequality/economic side of *oikos*, I have been promoting four main ideas:

1) universal basic income
2) shorter working week
3) open borders
4) progressive global wealth tax

In many ways, these are all interlinked. On the ecological damage/climate change side of *oikos*, we should consider:

1) full commitment to renewable energies – breaking free of fossil fuels
2) speaking out prophetically to educate about the externalisation of costs
3) living within our fair share of the world's resources – promoting local plant-based diets, appropriate travel, and small environmental footprints
4) using power as voter, consumer, and investor to prioritise relationships with fellow human beings and with nature.

Across the spectrum of ideas
The prisoner's dilemma facing countries is that if they, and they alone, take action, they could be worse off. Monetary and fiscal policies are not the route to a new equilibrium. So with interest rates close to zero, and fiscal policy

constrained by high government debt, the objective of economic policy for many countries is to lower the exchange rate. There is a real risk of a 'currency war'. International cooperation instead is essential. Placing obligations on surplus countries has not and will not work. Instead, King wants to aim: (a) to reinvigorate the IMF and reinforce its legitimacy by reforms to its voting system; (b) to put in place a permanent system of swap agreements among central banks; (c) to accept floating exchange rates; and (d) to return to normal real interest rates. The leaderships of the United Nations and the IMF must raise their games (King, 2016).

Hickel feels a crucial step towards creating a fairer global economy would be to actually democratise the major institutions of global governance: the World Bank, the IMF and the WTO – abolishing the veto power of the United States, and going with one vote to each country. Monbiot would prefer to scrap the IMF, the WTO and the World Bank. He wants to start again with a Fair Trade Organisation, an International Clearing Union and a World Parliament. A reconstituted United Nations should facilitate a progressive wealth fund of approximately $25 trillion annually from the asset rich. This global fund will allow the supranational institutions to distribute a universal basic income completely independent of national governments and improve equality of opportunity. Individual governments will continue to run their own tax and monetary policies adjusting as necessary to take into account the effects of a universal basic income.

Berry would not agree that these changes are enough to solve the world's problems. He, like Kate Raworth, wants to go much further:

Industrial destructiveness is our modern disease. If we were somehow granted a limitless supply of cheap, clean energy, we would continue our destruction of the world by agricultural erosion, chemical poisoning, industrial war, industrial recreation and various forms of 'development'. Epic feats of engineering require only a few brilliant technicians and a lot of money. But feeding a world of people year on year for a long time requires cultures of husbandry fitted to the nature of millions of unique small places – precisely the kind of cultures that industrialism has purposely disvalued, uprooted and destroyed. The future of food is not distinguishable from the future of the land, which in turn is indistinguishable from the future of human care. The issue of food distribution is as important as food production. But past models of agricultural production need not limit us from seeing new and alternative ways of feeding nine billion people living mainly in cities – e.g. more of a plant-based diet, protein from mass factories of insects and avoiding food waste. It depends ultimately on the health, not of the financial system, but of the ecosphere. Local adaption is not the work of a few; it is work for everybody, requiring everybody's intelligence. It is work inherently democratic. (Berry, 2017).

Berry suggests his ideas:

1. We must not work or think on a heroic scale. We must not break things we cannot fix. There is no justification, ever, for permanent ecological damage.
2. *We must abandon the delusion that the damages done by industrialization can be corrected by more industrialization.*
3. *We must quit solving our problems by 'moving on' – stay put geographically, historically and ecologically.*
4. *We must learn the sources and costs of our own economic lives.*
5. *We must give up the notion that we are too good to do our own work and clean up our own messes. It is not acceptable for this work to be done for us by wage slavery or by enslaving nature.*
6. *By way of correction, we must make local, locally adapted economies, and based on local nature, local sunlight, local intelligence and local work.*
7. *We must understand that these measures are radical and personal. They cannot be performed for us by any expert, political leader or corporation* (Berry, 2017).

Wendell Berry is hard to pigeon-hole: on one hand he seems an arch-right leaning conservative with his anti-urbanisation, anti-industrialisation stance; but on the other hand with his assaults on big money, markets and agri-business, he is more of a lefty environmentalist. In fact, his main villain is the 'American Dream' (unrestrained capitalism). There are arguments against Berry's outlook – both practical and philosophical. Practically, what works well in rural Kentucky will not solve the problem of feeding an overpopulated planet. Philosophically, consumer materialism is about all the Western world's poorer classes have left to look forward to. Will the future force us all to live in smaller societies without the internal combustion engine, as Berry's book *The World-Ending Fire* suggests? Perhaps Wendell Berry will have the last laugh but by then there may not be much to laugh about! God can encompass 'limitlessness', but human beings cannot!

Pinker tries to be positive again:

> 'As societies have become healthier, wealthier, freer, happier, and
> better educated, they have set their sights on the most pressing
> global challenges. They have emitted fewer pollutants, cleared fewer
> forests, spilled less oil, set aside more preserves, extinguished fewer
> species, saved the ozone layer, and peaked in their consumption of
> oil, farmland, timber, paper, cars, coal and perhaps even carbon.
> For all their differences, the world's nations came to a historic
> agreement on climate change, as they did in previous years on
> nuclear testing, proliferation, security and disarmament. Nuclear
> weapons, since the extraordinary circumstances of the closing days
> of World War II, have not been used in the seventy odd years they
> have existed. Nuclear terrorism, in defiance of forty years of expert
> predictions, has never happened. The world's nuclear stockpiles
> have been reduced by 85%, with more reductions to come, and
> testing has ceased (except in North Korea?) and proliferation has
> frozen' (Pinker, 2018).

In Pinker's view, two of the world's most pressing problems, then, though not yet solved, are solvable: practicable long-term agendas have been laid out for eliminating nuclear weapons and for mitigating climate change (Pinker, 2018). Transformative ideas are originating from psychology, ecology, physics, history, earth system science, geography, architecture, sociology and complexity science. Economics would be wise to embrace these. The financial crisis has turned economics into an issue of public discussion and debate. Everyone should draw on their rich bank of experience as a personal reference point for sense-checking the morality of the economic theories that abound (Raworth, 2017).

Social morality

Dr Norman Hamilton, Presbyterian Minister, has raised concern that morality often seems limited to issues of personal morality. This is not a biblical or Christian view of morality. He believes in social morality. He suggested that it is a profoundly moral question to ask whether states should borrow ever more billions, since the repayment of those loans will fall on future generations who had no say in the decision to borrow in the first place! Many question the morality of why it seems acceptable for farmers to receive 46p for two litres of milk, while consumers pay 89p in the shops for it – and willingly hand over £1 for a two litre bottle of Coca-Cola (Hamilton, 2017).

Economics is more than two thousand years behind medicine in honing its ethics. But as economics profoundly influences the lives of us all, it must act in service (to human prosperity), respect autonomy (with engagement and consent), be prudential (minimise the risk of harm) and work with humility. There is a striking degree of deeply held independence (not quite selfishness) in the Land of Plenty that believes in self-provision: private cars rather than public transport, private house ownership rather than rented accommodation. This in turn has bred a neoliberal suspicion of publicly funded services. Whatever the public/private split, better that local and global economies are transformed to make them distributive and regenerative by design (Raworth, 2017).

Ruth Sanderson, a Northern Ireland based journalist, also writing in the Presbyterian Herald, is full of righteous anger:

> *I feel livid at the vitriol spewed out by some of the right-wing press, a growing acceptance that it is okay to turn away migrants, or that they are in some way part of the reason why economies fail or 'local' people cannot get jobs. I feel angry that while all this venom festers, the super-rich become richer and the bottom billion continues to die of war, hunger and avoidable diseases.*
>
> *We are bedevilled by politeness. No one likes to make himself or herself a nuisance, lest they be branded 'difficult'. Well, it's not about being liked; it's about doing what is right. In circumstances when we encounter great injustice, 'difficult' might get things done.*
>
> *In the wake of recent world events, I have heard many Christians shrug their shoulders helplessly and say, 'Oh well, God is sovereign' in a very resigned way. Of course God is sovereign, that is not up for debate. However, God's sovereignty must not be an excuse for indifference. If we are the outworking of God's plans for the world and see things happening that are just plain wrong, then we have a moral duty to take action. Moreover, Christians should be the ones leading this action. We are God's arms, legs and mouths in the world and He wants to use us. This means speaking out when we encounter issues which jar with what is right (Sanderson, 2017).*

Migrants

With inequality so great across the world, it is no wonder, then, that millions of people have come knocking on the gates of the Land of Plenty. In the nineteenth century, inequality was still a matter of class; nowadays, it is a matter of location. An American earns eight times as much for the same work as a Nigerian, even when they are of the same skill level, age and sex (Bregman, 2018). It's apartheid on a global scale. Bregman is keen to expose the common fallacies about migrants:

1. They are all terrorists
2. They are all criminals
3. They all undermine social cohesion
4. They will take our jobs
5. Cheap immigrant labour will force our wages down
6. They are too lazy to work
7. They will never go back (Bregman, 2018).

None of these statements are true. Travel is expensive, and few people in very poor countries can afford to emigrate; even so, 700 million people would prefer to move to a different country (Gallop World Poll, 2018). Why are thousands of people risking drowning in the Mediterranean Sea, trying to get into Europe from Africa or the Middle East, and paying traffickers over $1,000 per head when they could fly for half that price? Well, due to an EU Directive, airlines are responsible for meeting the cost of returning anyone to their country of origin that is declared to be an illegal immigrant. And why are the boats so unseaworthy? Well, all craft are confiscated at European ports on arrival – one-way trip only! Humans didn't evolve by staying in one place. Wanderlust is in the blood. However disruptive it may be, migration has time and time again proven to be one of the most powerful drivers of progress. However, the Land of Plenty remains locked and barred. Article 13 of the Universal Declaration of Human Rights says everyone has the right to leave their country, but guarantees no one the right to move to the Land of Plenty. If all the developed world countries would let in just three per cent more immigrants, the world's poor would have £305 billion more to spend (Walmsley et al, 2007; Bregman, 2018)

Reducing inequality will mean important sacrifices, financial and otherwise, as we try to battle social injustice. Rather than only making gestures as individuals, our impact will be much greater if we can take whole nations along with us to a **more realistic standard of living**. Thereby there is the real prospect of helping to balance out inequalities across the world at least a little.

Tech-haves and tech-have-nots

Bartlett outlines both 'utopian' and 'dystopian' visions. A growing number of people from both the left and the right of politics imagine that the falling cost of goods and higher machine-driven productivity will produce a world of plenty and the end of meaningless work. Our lives will be happier, easier, and more fulfilling: a utopia driven by a universal basic income. By contrast, the dystopian scenario is that central governments will gradually lose the ability to function properly. Inequality will rapidly increase even further to a point where a tiny number of people end up with all of 'the tech' and all the wealth and everyone else has no choice but to scratch out a living serving these winners. A third possibility involves a more slowly growing inequality, which at present seems unavoidable, leading to the worsening of many social problems, including depression, alcoholism and crime. And yet simultaneously the tax base would be falling, due to the gig economy, offshore monopolies, tax havens and crypto-currencies.

The social side effect of growing inequality would be an increasingly fractured society composed of different social and ethnic groups whose jobs, schools or paths never cross, online or off. One predictable new fault line of inequality could be between the tech-haves who enjoy the benefits of personal AI bots, high productivity and stupendous healthcare, and a less savvy underclass. What if economic growth in the future no longer depended on individual freedom and entrepreneurial spirit, but on capital and the ownership of smart machines that can drive research? Bartlett fears 'universal basic income' wouldn't be a dreamy utopia of satisfied and empowered citizens, but instead a very neat way for millionaires to keep the poorest in society from rebelling. These seem like the dangerous circumstances required for democracy to dip towards some new flavour of authoritarianism. The idea of democracy won't disappear, but it would be little more than a shell system, where real power and authority is increasingly centralised and run by a small group of techno-wizards (Bartlett, 2018).

Rather, we have to break down the power of the experts – whether economists or technologists. Let's follow innovators who are evolving the economy one experiment at a time in the proven dynamism of the collaborative commons, and in the vast potential of regenerative design. We remake the economy by moving our savings to ethical banks; enshrining living purpose in the enterprises we set up; contributing to the knowledge commons; and campaigning with political movements that share this economic vision (Raworth, 2017).

Anti-inequality

Despite being an expert economist, Sir Tony Atkinson was keen on innovation and new ideas. Crucially, Professor Atkinson did not accept that rising inequality is inevitable: it is not solely the product of forces outside our control. There are steps that can be taken by governments, acting individually or collectively, by firms, by trade unions and consumer organisations, and by us as individuals to reduce the present levels of inequality. He did not discuss, in his book, investment in education and training which is important and complementary to the fifteen more radical measures he did propose. The fifteen proposals are summarised below:

P1 The direction of technological change should be an explicit concern of policy-makers, encouraging innovation in a form that increases the employability of workers and emphasises the human dimension of service provision.

P2 Public policy should aim for a proper balance of power among stakeholders, and to this end (a) introduce an explicitly distributional dimension into competition policy; (b) ensure a legal framework that allows trade unions to represent workers on level terms; and (c) establish, where it does not already exist, a Social and Economic Council involving the social partners and other nongovernmental bodies.

P3 The government should adopt an explicit target for preventing and reducing unemployment and underpin this ambition by offering guaranteed public employment at the minimum wage to those who seek it.

P4 There should be a national pay policy, consisting of two elements: a statutory minimum wage set at a living wage, and a code of practice for pay above the minimum, agreed as part of a 'national conversation' involving a Social and Economic Council.

P5 The government should offer, via national savings bonds, a guaranteed positive real rate of interest on savings, with a maximum holding per person.

P6 There should be a capital endowment (minimum inheritance) paid to all at adulthood.

P7 A public Investment Authority should be created, operating a sovereign wealth fund with the aim of building up the net worth of the state by holding investments in companies and in property.

P8 We should return to a more progressive rate structure for personal income tax, with marginal rates of tax increasing by ranges of taxable income, up to a top rate of sixty-five per cent, accompanied by a broadening of the tax base.

P9 The government should introduce into the personal income tax an Earned Income Discount, limited to the first band of earnings.

P10 Receipts of inheritance and gifts inter vivos should be taxed under a progressive lifetime capital receipts tax.

P11 There should be a proportional, or progressive, property tax based on up-to-date property assessments.

P12 Child benefit should be paid for all children at a substantial rate and should be taxed as income.

P13 A Participation Income should be introduced at a national level, complementing existing social protection, with the prospect of a worldwide child basic income or even a universal basic income.

P14 (Alternative to 13): There should be a renewal of social insurance, raising the level of benefits and extending their coverage.

P15 Rich countries should raise their target for Official Development Aid to one per cent of Gross National Income.

Atkinson also has some other ideas he thought were worth considering:

Idea 1: A thoroughgoing review of the access of households to the credit market for borrowing not secured on housing.
Idea 2: Examination of the case for an 'income-tax-based' treatment of contributions to private pensions, along the lines of present 'privileged' saving schemes, which would bring forward the payment of tax.
Idea 3: A re-examination of the case for an annual wealth tax and the prerequisites for its successful introduction to fund sovereign wealth funds.
Idea 4: A global tax regime for personal taxpayers, based on total wealth.
Idea 5: A minimum tax for corporations. (Atkinson, 2015).

The proposals and ideas are bold, but bold measures are required if we are to return to the degree of egalitarianism that existed before the 'Inequality Turn' in the 1980s. There has to be an appetite for action, and this requires political leadership. The interrelation between inequality and politics is critical. A major instrumental reason for concern about economic inequality is that concentrations of wealth and income convey political power and influence (see A C Grayling and Chapter 7). The political message has been couched in the corrosive view that there is nothing that can be done: that there is no alternative to the present high levels of inequality. In agreement with Piketty, Atkinson rejected this view because there have been periods in the past, not just in wartime, when significant reductions in inequality and poverty were achieved.

The United Kingdom is perhaps waking up to the urgent need for economic change. The Institute of Public Policy Research (IPPR) Commission on Economic Justice Report 2018 was published in the autumn of the same year, entitled 'Prosperity and Justice: A plan for the new economy'. The executive summary highlighted ten key messages. Of most interest, perhaps, was message number seven: spreading wealth and ownership access across the economy by, for example, the establishment of a Citizens' (sovereign) Wealth Fund for the whole UK population, to provide a small annual dividend for everyone; and number eight: designing simpler, fairer and more progressive taxes such as a lifetime gifts tax levied on the recipient.

The twenty-first century is different, notably in the nature of the labour market and in the globalisation of the economy, but we can learn from history when looking to the future and in doing so prove the aforementioned G W F Hegel wrong. Are calls for healthcare to change from "absolutely free at the point of delivery" and at the same time calls for a "universal basic income" completely contradictory? I don't think so. Both themes introduce the concept of individual stewardship. Completely free health care tends to lead to profligate use and weakens public health messages. Individuals targeting the spending of a universal basic income, in partnership with state welfare provision, on their priority health needs will develop the skills of stewardship. And good stewardship will undoubtedly be needed by all of us in the future: both in combating inequality and in mitigating ecological impact.

Transnational challenges

Fara Dabhoiwala, in *The Guardian*, December 2018, reviews Sophia Rosenfeld's book *Democracy and Truth: A Short History*:

> *What history shows is that democracy depends on a shared recommitment to verifiable truth and truth-telling ... that allows societies to harmonise expert knowledge and popular sense for the common good. Rosenfeld agrees with Klein and feels the story of modern democracy is also the story of modern capitalism and has*

allowed the moral failure of our economic system. The more we are divided by gross and growing inequality, the harder it becomes to find the common ground on which our politics depends. Democratic politics is also, by and large, national politics … But the biggest challenges of our time are transnational. Nation state policies are largely irrelevant and a hindrance to tackling global challenges' (Rosenfeld in Dabhoiwala, 2018).

One important lesson is that action needs to be taken across the whole range of government. Policy to combat inequality and poverty cannot be delegated to one county council, one ministry department, or to one agency of the United Nations or the IMF. However, in the meantime much of the 'heavy lifting' will fall to national governments. Obviously, previously, many government initiatives have ended in abject failure. But this has often been due to lack of prior planning and consultation. And it is individuals who ultimately determine whether proposals are implemented and ideas pursued. They will do so as voters, and in the future, indirectly, as lobbyists, through campaign groups and social media. Individuals can also influence the extent of inequality in society directly by their own actions as consumers, as savers, as investors, as workers or as employers. This is most evident in terms of individual philanthropy, where transfers of resources not only are valuable in themselves but also provide a powerful signal of what we should like to see done by our governments. In our economic lives, as well as our personal lives, we make many ethical decisions, and – taken together – our decisions can make a contribution to reducing the extent of inequality.

The achievement of a less unequal society in the period of World War II and subsequent post-war decades has not been fully overthrown. At a global level, the great divergence between countries following the Industrial Revolution is closing. It is true that since 1980 we have seen an 'Inequality Turn' in the Western world and that the twenty-first century brings challenges in terms of the ageing of the population, climate change and not-yet-addressed global imbalances.

Hickel feels a vital step would be to make the international trade system fairer. Instead of requiring across-the-board tariff reductions, trade could be conducted with an intentional bias towards poor countries, for the sake of promoting development. Also making free trade agreements public and open to real democratic scrutiny would help. Shortening patent durations and securing exemptions for essential goods, including seeds, plants and genetic materials, would be important for small farmers across the Global

South. Finally, the agricultural subsidy regime needs reform. Subsidies in the rich world should be ended but subsidies for small farmers in the South are still essential to curb hunger (Hickel, 2017).

But the solutions to these problems lie in our own hands. If we are willing to use today's greater wealth to address these challenges, and accept that resources should be shared less unequally, then there are indeed grounds for optimism (Atkinson, 2015).

Look up AND around

However, King feels that since the 2008 crisis there is also a new pessimism about the ability of market economies today to generate prosperity. But the era of great discoveries has not necessarily come to an end. Some countries have experienced buoyant population growth and rising participation in the labour force. Economists have a poor track record in predicting demographic changes that can lead to progress.

The paradox of policy applies to all countries, both those that previously consumed and borrowed too much and those that spent too little. Mervyn King suggests that a reform programme might comprise three elements: first, the development of measures to boost productivity (a shorter working week?); second, the promotion of trade (fair free trade?); and third, the restoration of floating exchange rates (King, 2016). This seems too limited – we need also to embrace all of Raworth's ideas for Doughnut Economics, reflect on the insights of Bregman, Kingsnorth and Berry, and take to heart the gentle guidance of Beynon.

Beynon reminds us from a Christian perspective that everything we have is from God's hand, rather than merely earned by ours. Anything we possess is from Him, and anything we give to Him is only returning it to Him. We are never self-made. We need to learn that, in fact, 'greed is good' doesn't work. The problem is that we find it is very hard to learn this. Jesus tells us to beware all kinds of greed. Greed restricts itself to no economic boundaries or salary levels. One way in which we can and should be different from Western consumerist culture is not to expect our standard of living always to go up as we go on through life (Beynon, 2011). C S Lewis also challenged our modern financial culture:

> *'If our expenditure on comforts, luxuries, amusements, etc. is up to the standard common among those with the same income as our own, we are probably giving away too little. If our charities do not pinch or hamper us, I should say they are too small. There*

ought to be things we should like to do and cannot because our charities expenditure (giving) excludes them'.

This is very hard to argue with. Unless, of course, you favour Pinker's post-Enlightenment views that the abandonment of religion and superstition has set humanity on a better path towards improvement, and that reason and science can replace religion. However, Jonathan Swift, indeed an Enlightenment product but also a Christian, in his writings had perhaps a keener awareness of the limitations of reason or the rational mind. *Gulliver's Travels* is an anatomy of human nature. The book asks readers to refute and deny that he has adequately characterised human nature and society. Each of the four parts – recounting four voyages to mostly fictional exotic lands – has a different theme, but all are attempts to deflate human pride. Critics hail the work as a reflection on the shortcomings of Enlightenment thought.

Even from a purely secular perspective, there is much to be concerned about. The lower middle classes, in rich countries, have seen their incomes rise by less than ten per cent in two decades. A fifth of the American population still believes that women should return to traditional roles, and a tenth is opposed to interracial dating. The country suffers from more than 3,000 hate crimes a year, and more than 15,000 homicides. Americans lose two hours a day to housework, and about a quarter of them feel they are always rushed. More than two thirds of Americans deny that they are very happy, around the same proportion as seventy years ago, and both women and men in the largest demographic age group have become unhappier over time. Every year around 40,000 Americans become so desperately unhappy that they take their own lives.

And, of course, the problems that span the entire planet are formidable. Before the century is out, it will have to accommodate another two billion people. A hundred million hectares of tropical rainforest were cut down in the previous decade. Marine fishes have declined by almost forty per cent, and thousands of species are threatened with extinction. Huge amounts of greenhouse gases – carbon dioxide and methane – enter the atmosphere every year, which, if left unchecked, threaten to raise global temperatures dangerously (Pinker, 2018). There is unevenness in carbon emissions that needs to be recognised. One could easily estimate the distribution of CO_2 emissions across the world's population by income group and not by country. The top ten per cent richest Americans, Luxembourgers, Singaporeans, and Saudi Arabians are the highest individual emitters in the world, with annual per capita emissions above $200tCO_2e$. At the other end of the pyramid of

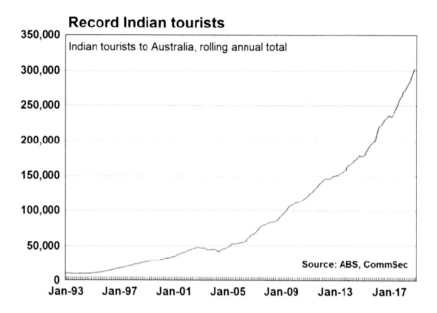

emitters lie the lowest income groups of Honduras, Mozambique, Rwanda and Malawi, with emissions 2,000 times lower, at around $0.1tCO_2e$ per person per year (Chancel and Piketty, 2015). It is sobering to review the trends in air travel tourism: in 1950, 0.1 billion flight passengers; in 1970, 0.2 billion flight passengers; in 2000, 0.7 billion flight passengers; and in 2017, 1.3 billion flight passengers. Exponential increase predicts 1.7 billion flight passengers for 2030 (UN World Tourism Organisation, 2017)! It is important to realise that a fine balancing act must be achieved between three variables: growth rates of poor (and populous) countries, migration, and environmental sustainability. In principle this will require large sacrifices from the rich – an especially unpopular proposition (Milanovic, 2016).

Nationally and internationally change is urgently needed in respect of how the 'haves' relate to the 'have-nots'. As stated above the United Nations needs to lead. However, on a personal level, how should we divide our own giving - individually, locally and globally?

Karl Marx attacked Christianity in part because he thought that it prevented people from tackling the social problems that were all around them, encouraging them instead to gaze passively into the sky, waiting for a saviour to come and rescue them. His critique had some point to it. Those who hear God's message are meant to respond by looking around them and acting, as Christ would do – to reach out to the needy. We are invited to look around, not only up (Nicholson, 2018).

Inside a parable

In *The Political Samaritan*, Nick Spencer (Director of Studies at the think tank Theos) contends that the one remaining piece of Scripture that still gets a political outing, at least in the UK, is the Parable of the Good Samaritan (Luke 10:25–37). He identifies its use across the political spectrum including the Thatcherite Samaritan, the Labour Samaritan (used by PMs Tony Blair and Gordon Brown) and the contemporary Samaritans (used by Nicola Sturgeon, Hilary Benn, Jeremy Corbyn, and Theresa May). The Good Samaritan is also deployed by backbenchers and frontbenchers in the UK parliament and in speeches and interviews elsewhere. He is deployed to justify economic policy; to vindicate military intervention; to defend overseas aid; to shape refugee, asylum and immigration policy; to preserve health provision; and to address international crises. He is also deployed to inspire moral universalism, to berate indifference and to condemn political opponents. But what does the Parable of the Good Samaritan actually mean? What is Jesus actually saying?

The answers to those questions are very far from being straightforward. Depending on how narrowly or widely you draw the circle, the parable is about how you interpret the Torah; how you interpret religious or ethical law more generally; how you should overcome religious division; how you should overcome ethical division; how you should not take your ethical status for granted; how you should be morally interventionist; how you should go the extra mile; how you should avoid fixating on legalism; how you should avoid seeing others as recipients of your ethical care but instead look first at yourself; how love does not allow limits on the definition of neighbour; how one cannot define one's neighbour but only be a neighbour; how we should eschew asking self-justifying ethical questions; how we can understand a model for God, humanity and salvation; and perhaps most importantly how we should stop asking and start doing! So the parable can mean quite a lot, actually. In good Christian fashion, what looks like a half-dead metaphor is, in fact, surprisingly and strangely alive (Spencer, 2018).

Giving

So how do we address our own giving if we are able? Should we help out individual acquaintances that are in financial difficulties? What if monies loaned are not paid back? Should church projects at home take precedence over those abroad? Which charities working overseas should benefit from our financial support? Do we give priority to secular or faith-based organisations working in areas of great poverty and need? How much giving should be targeted at long-term development and how much at short-term immediate aid?

In both the Old Testament and the New Testament, we see examples of whom money was given to. In the Old Testament there is a focus on the poor who are fellow Israelites:

> 'If anyone is poor among your fellow Israelites in any of the towns of the land that the Lord your God is giving you, do not be hard-hearted or tight-fisted towards them. Rather, be open-handed and freely lend them whatever they need' (Deuteronomy 15:7–8)

However, God's people were also to care for the foreigners among them:

> 'The foreigner residing among you must be treated as your native-born. Love them as yourself, for you were foreigners in Egypt. I am the Lord your God' (Leviticus 19:33–34)

We see much the same in the New Testament. First, there is care for those in need:

> '… There was no needy person among them. For from time to time those who owned land or houses sold them, brought the money from the sales and put it at the apostles' feet, and it was distributed to anyone who had need' (Acts 4:34–35)

The care here is primarily within the Christian community because of the new relationship between Christians. But secondly, care can, and should, overflow to those outside the church as well. So Paul says:

> 'Therefore, as we have opportunity, let us do good to all people…'
> (Galatians 6:10)

What will this mean in practice? Think of expanding circles of personal giving:
- Care for those within our own church
- Care between churches across the world
- Care for others in our locality
- Care for others elsewhere in the world

Some suggest giving a precise percentage – usually ten per cent of our income ('tithing'). Of course, now we live in modern states, and not in Old Testament Israel, and some of this money in Israel would have gone towards what is now covered by government taxes and redistribution through welfare state provision. Taxes (from those who pay them) contribute towards care of those who are poor or ill (which should give a new meaning to taxes – they are part of caring for those around us). Another problem of tithing is hidden in the mathematics: a tithe on a £6,000 annual income leaves £5,400 for personal spending, a tithe on a £60,000 annual income leaves £54,000 for personal spending and a tithe on a £600,000 annual income leaves £540,000 – not really equitable. However, some need to be honest: if some incomes were reduced by ten per cent then those of us in the top decile of the income distribution would actually manage life fine. Graham Beynon suggests giving should be thoughtful, regular, and secret (Beynon, 2011). We do need a **revalued standard of living/lifestyle**.

Graham Beynon perhaps focuses too much on the individual without enough thought towards the wider societal and global impact of how we spend our money. There is no attempt to learn from the approaches towards money of Christians in other cultures, so it is fair to ask therefore how much of what he advises is British culture rather than Kingdom culture.

Democratising globalisation

Stiglitz believes that in order to make globalisation work, we will have to think and act more globally. Seldom is global policy discussed in terms of social justice. There is pretence that there are no trade-offs – no negative externalities. The ingredients of a new global social contract include:

- A commitment to a fairer trade regime
- A new approach to intellectual property promoting research
- Compensating countries for their environmental services
- Everyone lowering carbon emissions
- Fair payment to developing countries for their natural resources
- Financial assistance of 0.7% GDP from all developed nations
- Debt forgiveness to prevent debt servicing transferring monies from poor to rich
- A global reserve system
- Force multinational corporations to confront their liabilities from damage to the environment
- Supporting democracy (Stiglitz, 2006)

Kate Raworth's final thoughts and conclusion are:

> *The Doughnut of social and planetary boundaries is a simple visualisation of the dual conditions that underpin collective*

human well-being. The social foundation demarks the Doughnut's inner boundary, and sets out the basics of life on which no one should be left falling short. The ecological ceiling demarks the Doughnut's outer boundary, beyond which humanity's pressure on Earth's life-giving systems is in dangerous overshoot. Between the two sets of boundaries lies the ecologically safe and socially just space in which humanity can thrive (Raworth, 2017).

Both Raworth and Pinker see two existential threats to humanity. They are in agreement regarding climate change, but Pinker worries about nuclear weapons whereas Raworth is more concerned with social injustice and inequality causing extreme poverty. God is all about giving and forgiving; many humans are all about getting and forgetting.

Limits of market economies

I agree with Kate Raworth and Naomi Klein that not everything should be left to the market and that applying a purely 'rational mind' to all economic conduct is problematic. Pure economic growth will not redress inequality and it will not solve the problem of pollution; and changing the predominant neoliberal mind-set through persuasion is not going to be easy. There is a role for what Klein calls 'Blockadia' – peaceful protest often inspired by indigenous peoples. And Raworth's ideas are just what campaigners need to feel confident to shout 'That's nonsense!' at the next economist they hear talking about essential GDP growth. Both women provide a clear guide to why traditional economic thinking helped to get us into this mess and how it is unlikely to help us out of it.

Sider (2015) states: '*Market economies have been far more successful than existing alternatives in creating wealth. Those who care about the poor should endorse carefully regulated market-orientated economies – rather than state-owned, centrally planned ones – as the best basic framework currently known for economic life*'. However, Sider feels that it does not mean we endorse a libertarian view that condemns virtually all government intervention in the economy. The mechanism of supply and demand pays no attention whatsoever to whether the purchaser wants to buy basic food or luxury items. The poorest billion have hardly any capital except their bodies. Every family should have basic capital – land, money, knowledge – to earn their own way, and be dignified, participating members of society.

The kinds of capital that people need vary with the situation. In a largely agricultural society, land reform is essential. This has to be undertaken with intelligence and certainly better thought through than was the case in Zimbabwe during the 1970s and 1980s, where land reform impoverished one of the great breadbaskets of Africa. In a largely information-based society, equality of educational opportunity will empower the poor. Money needed to buy a house, start a small business, or prepare for retirement is important; this can be funded through both private voluntary programmes and the activities of democratic governments. Microfinance is growing due to a global effort, but it is not the silver bullet to end all poverty. So far, there is only a limited increase in entrepreneurial activity and no measurable decrease in poverty rates (Kendall and Voorhies, 2014). But some distinguished development specialists continue to recommend microloans (Conway, 2012). Recent innovations in cell phone technology make it possible to transfer money directly to a poor person's cell phone account (ninety per cent coverage) (Kendall and Voorhies, 2014). GiveDirectly gave a sample of thatched-roof households in East Africa a one-time gift of $1,000. This resulted in a 33% drop in days children went without food and a 116% increase in household investment in land, farm inputs, livestock and housing (GiveDirectly, 2012). More benefits should be seen over the next ten and twenty years. Social entrepreneurs can use disciplines of the corporate world (rigorous assessment of results, adaption, innovation and risk taking) to solve social problems (Bornstein and Davis, 2010).

Tiny entrepreneurs cannot flourish if they lack fair legal systems, reliable infrastructure, wise macroeconomic policies, and public systems of education and health care. What works and what doesn't? We must avoid centralised power. Economist Michael Todaro insists that 'public–private cooperation', and not the triumph of free market and laissez-fair economics, is the real lesson of the success stories of the Asian Tigers (Todaro, 1994). The South Korean and Taiwan miracle started with government-organised, effective and fair land reform, and better health, education and job training. Half of the growth resulted from the state's investment in education and technical skills to make the most of recent technologies (Dreze and Sen (1989) coined the term 'participatory growth'). Governments turned against protectionism and refused to protect their nations' companies from international competition once they had achieved a certain level of maturity.

Brazil, during its rapid economic growth (what Dreze and Sen termed 'unaimed opulence'), did not invest in health care and education so tens of millions of poor Brazilians remained stuck in poverty. Until, that is, President da Silva launched the Zero Hunger Programme and the Bolsa Familia Programme targeted at the poorest families with conditional cash grants. A vibrant market economy then produced economic empowerment of the poor, and extreme poverty in Brazil dropped from ten per cent to two per cent of the total population. The World Bank now believes governments should do less where markets work and do more where they don't.

If the economy is growing, is society improving? This is an absurd notion. Divorce, environmental pollution, crime, smoking, alcoholism, gambling, prostitution and pornography all drive up GDP! And anyway, GDP measures only money changing hands; it does not count unpaid work in the family or the community at all. There are echoes here of Bernard Mandeville, the eighteenth-century doctor/psychologist, contending that morality is a construct when he states in *The Fable of the Bees* that public benefit derives from private vice. Rather, the Redefining Progress organisation has, in modern times as mentioned earlier, developed a Genuine Progress Indicator, which measures more than twenty things that GDP ignores, including housework and volunteering. The GPI counts a nation's use of non-renewable resources and goods, which perish quickly in the same way a private business does, as a loss (Venetoulis and Cubb, 2004)!

In almost all countries, after an initial rise of GPI as GDP increased, the GPI has levelled off or even declined. For example, in China, GPI is now declining due to pollution, the depletion of non-renewable resources, crime and family breakdown. Since the Enlightenment, the autonomous individual has replaced God as the source of ethics. The scientific method became the only avenue to truth. Tragically, this new view abandons the limits on economic growth imposed by historical Christian faith and in turn devastates family, community life and the environment. While not answering fundamental questions, GPI or other such indexes will make it easier for us to think carefully. Even the UN has formally endorsed the Human Development Index (HDI), a somewhat simpler index, using the three metrics of GDP, literacy and life expectancy.

Enoughism

It is idolatrous nonsense to suggest that human fulfilment comes from an ever-increasing supply of material things. It hardens our hearts to the cries of the poor. Christian joy is in Jesus Christ, not rising affluence where people consume more and more to keep pace with their neighbours but never attain their distant, urgently sought goal. We must develop a 'theology of enough' in response to a 'theology of poverty'. Brandon Robshaw, in *The Independent*, February 1, 2009, reviews *Times* journalist John Naish's book, *Enough: Breaking Free from the World of Excess*. Naish's thesis is that we in the affluent West have more than enough of what we need, yet cannot stop gorging ourselves, both literally and metaphorically. Having evolved in a world where there was never quite enough food, we are hard-wired to grab it whenever we get the chance; now we live in the midst of plenty but the instinct is still there. We evolved to be curious about the world we live in; now, surrounded by information, we can't stop reading our emails, checking our texts, watching telly, surfing the net. Our need to accumulate possessions has created a wasteful, consumerist society with disastrous consequences both for our souls and for the environment. But, says Naish, we can fight back. Our rational selves can overcome those lower-brain urges. If we follow the philosophy of 'Enoughism', consciously limiting our consumption, there is hope for us yet. We must develop models of simpler lifestyles; corporate policies that permit people to choose parenting, leisure and community service; and promote advertising practices that discourage overconsumption.

Rather, a 'poverty of theology' allows consumerism to roll on unchallenged or weakly challenged by faith communities. Structures advocating greater pollution control often only benefit the middle classes at the expense of the poor. So we need the compassion to embrace long-term structural changes if displaced workers (due to reduced demand) are to find other roles in societies that care for all people. Developed nations should gradually eliminate trade barriers on imports from the developing world. Without trade barriers, we could buy sustainably produced imported goods more cheaply and developing countries could increase both their production and income via increased exports, especially in goods that should only be produced in the tropics. We should work to make all trade freer and fairer. Yet year after year, the Doha round of trade negotiations has failed to make progress. Powerful organisations fight back to protect their narrow self-interests. But adjustment assistance and system reform is required by governments so that some sacrifices by rich Northerners can produce major benefits in the Global South. There will be costs whether we go the 0.7% ODA route, the universal basic income route or the open borders route.

Labour and capital

Democratic institutions must be encouraged, civil society strengthened and free trade unions nurtured to improve working conditions and avoid elites seizing all the benefits. All large corporations need to endorse the International Labour Organisation's conventions. **The eight fundamental Conventions are:**

1. Freedom of Association and Protection of the Right to Organise Convention, 1948 (No. 87)
2. Right to Organise and Collective Bargaining Convention, 1949 (No. 98)
3. Forced Labour Convention, 1930 (No. 29)
4. Abolition of Forced Labour Convention, 1957 (No. 105)
5. Minimum Age Convention, 1973 (No. 138)
6. Worst Forms of Child Labour Convention, 1999 (No. 182)
7. Equal Remuneration Convention, 1951 (No. 100)
8. Discrimination (Employment and Occupation) Convention, 1958 (No. 111)

The four governance Conventions are:

1. Labour Inspection Convention, 1947 (No. 81)
2. Employment Policy Convention, 1964 (No. 122)
3. Labour Inspection (Agriculture) Convention, 1969 (No. 129)
4. Tripartite Consultation (International Labour Standards) Convention, 1976 (No. 144)

Just wages demand a global minimum wage. Perhaps setting the bar at fifty per cent of a country's median wage, or at least above the national poverty line, would be a good start. The UN's International Labour Organisation claims to have the capacity to govern such a system (Hickel, 2017).

Hickel also wants to improve domestic tax collection by starting globally to change the WTO's customs invoicing standards, to prevent transfer mispricing and to close down tax havens in a drive for global financial transparency. Revealing the 'beneficial owners' of all companies, trusts and foundations would allow their income and wealth to be taxed by their home countries or the United Nations. The Tax Justice Network has already succeeded in getting some initial reforms enacted by national governments. On the land front, the global network of small farmers known as La Via Campesina is organising against land grabs, agri-business monopolies and seed patents. Real momentum against climate change is building in unexpected ways, with Native Americans using their territorial rights to block fossil fuel projects and students pressing their universities to divest from fossil fuels (Hickel, 2017).

Consumers can have influence in this area with conscientious decisions about what and where to buy. Multinational corporations' global reach means that no one country can regulate them in the absence of a new Fair Trade

Organisation. It is not acceptable in global trade negotiations for MNCs to have ninety-two delegates, trade associations sixteen delegates, trade unions two delegates, and environmental groups only one representative! Alldred confirmed that when he was a member of the Irish delegation to the WTO's 5th Ministerial Conference in Hong Kong in 2005, there were 528 US delegates accredited, 487 EU delegates accredited – and just 5 from the four cotton-producing countries of Chad, Niger, Mali and Burkina Faso (Alldred, personal communication, 2018). People representing the interests of workers and the environment must play a far more important role in all international trade negotiations.

All people should embrace 'ethical investing' and shareholders should protest against unjust corporate action. Boycotts of irresponsible businesses are useful civic actions. Although I am not an enthusiastic fan, sustained public protest can change even huge multi national corporations.

All steps have costs. I hesitate to make too many specific suggestions as these have been covered in comprehensive detail in *There is No Planet B* by Mike Berners-Lee; but changes will require action at every level:

- Walk, bike, carpool, and use public transport
- Reduce, reuse and recycle
- Use fuel efficient vehicles
- Avoid subsidised parking
- Use airplanes less
- Eat less red meat and dairy products
- Cut all greenhouse gas emissions
- Generate and research renewable energy (keep fossil fuels underground)
- Phase in carbon taxes at all levels
- Uphold international standards on pollution
- Reduce global poverty and therefore stop damage to marginal lands.

The average developed nation's overseas aid effort is only 0.45% of Gross National Income – really very stingy. Yes, industrialised nations expanded their foreign aid by 275% from 2001 to 2010 and therefore sub-Saharan Africa experienced some progress in human development (less poverty, better health). But William Easterly (Professor of Economics at New York University) argues that much Western foreign aid has been wasted because of a top down approach that has failed to understand what is needed on the ground (Easterly, 2006). Varying degrees of corruption, overheads and incompetence in developing countries siphoned off large amounts into tax havens. We need to improve the ways we give aid by working with 'searchers' who carefully explore what works concretely in local settings. Until global economic structural change occurs, the effectiveness of official development assistance needs to be **increased** by:

- Focusing on the poorest of the poor
- Promoting effective transparent governmental institutions free from corruption
- Focusing on empowerment, ending the violation of human rights
- Deemphasising the donors' political and economic interests
- Nurturing economic sustainability
- Emphasising developing country ownership – local decisions (for example 'Feed the Future')
- Separating development aid from military aid (and reduce military aid) … and
- Emphasising better education, nutrition and health care for women and children.

The plight of over a billion poor people today is more desperate than that of war-ravaged Europe during the Marshall Plan in the 1940s (Sider, 2015). It's when our political, ideological, or religious ideas are at stake that we become the most stubborn. Intelligent people are highly practised in finding arguments, experts and studies that underpin their pre-existing beliefs. Bregman asks whether new ideas can genuinely change the world. Well, Simon Kuznets willed the idea of GDP into being and the 'randomistas' upset the apple cart of foreign aid by forcing it to prove its efficacy. Political scientists have established that how people vote is determined less by their perceptions about their own lives than by their conceptions of society. We cast our vote not just for ourselves but also for the group or tribe we want to belong to.

Windows to the future
Perhaps it really is worth continuing to build new castles in the sky – their time may eventually come. The Austrian philosopher, Friedrich Hayek, and the American economist, Milton Friedman, were two people who dedicated their lives to building castles in the sky. Their big solution to just about every problem was the idea, at the time a radical one, of the free market. After World War II, reconstruction efforts were coloured by Keynesian ideas – the war state became the welfare state. Later as 'stagflation' occurred in Western

economies, as Friedman had predicted, he helped precipitate a global policy transformation of neoliberalism. However, the fact that our most heroic social justice movements in the past (abolition of slavery, universal suffrage) won on the legal front but suffered big losses on the economic front is precisely why our world is as fundamentally unequal and unfair as it remains (Klein, 2014). There is a great dearth of equality of opportunity – some have been born with their proverbial silver spoon but many have no form of cutlery at all!

> 'The rise of neoliberalism played out like a relay race, with think tanks passing the baton to journalists, who handed it off to politicians. Nowadays neither the political left nor the political right seem to have a very clear plan for the future; neoliberal ideas seem to have put a lockdown on the development of new ones in 'the end of history'. But ideas, however outrageous, have changed the world' (Bregman, 2018).

A universal basic income, a shorter workweek, a progressive global tax on capital and a world without borders … are all crazy dreams. They are four ideas outside the 'Overton Window'. The difficult question, for political resolution, remains how much should the 'haves' relinquish to give the 'have-nots' a decent standard of living. A full commitment to renewable energy, understanding the externalisation of costs, living within the biosphere's capacity and prioritising all relationships (human and ecological) are another four radical ideas to allow us all to have a revalued standard of living – economically, ecologically, ethically, morally and spiritually.

Hickel has his vision of a better future:

> Poor countries are liberated from the shackles of structural adjustment; they win an equal voice in the institutions of global governance; and the rules of international trade are rebalanced to give them a fair shot. All of a sudden they find themselves free to determine their own economic policies in their own national interests, without threat of coercion or invasion, and they resort to the developmentalist agenda that worked so well for them in the 1960s and 1970s. They nationalise their oil reserves and mines, and they reclaim control over their telecommunications and water infrastructure. They protect their domestic industries with strong tariffs, and nurture companies until they can compete effectively on the world stage. They break up the big foreign agribusinesses,

ensure that small farmers have stable access to land, and offer subsidies to promote national food security. As domestic industries grow, more jobs are created, labour unions win decent salaries for workers and a middle class begins to rise. Income growth rates inch their way up, poverty falls and hunger becomes a thing of the past. With the tax havens closed, government revenues increase and – without a crushing debt burden to pay off – there is room for social spending on universal health care and education. Universities increase their enrolment and, with better health systems and access to generic medicines, tropical diseases are kept in check at last (Hickel, 2017).

In the final analysis, Wendell Berry, Paul Kingsnorth, Naomi Klein, Ron Sider, George Monbiot, Jason Hickel and Graham Beynon have as much to say in their own way about a fairer, sustainable world as Mervyn King, Rutger Bregman, Steven Pinker, Chris Hughes, Anthony Atkinson, Thomas Piketty and Kate Raworth. A recent sermon mini-series by the Reverend Richard Gregg, Presbyterian Minister, was entitled 'Important Last Words'. The message from the end of the Old Testament was '....*keep on going – do not give up because there will be healing*' (Malachi 4:2) and from the end of the New Testament was '.... *I (Alpha and Omega) am coming soon to usher in My Kingdom*' (Revelation 22:7, 22:12–13, 22:20). Christians are called to be Kingdom people <u>now</u> and not only in the future. People see what they want – more household convenience, faster communications, cheaper food, wider travel – and get it by manipulating nature and its resources in any way possible. Never mind the price paid by others who are unseen. It is this inequality in how the marvellous bounty of planet Earth is shared out that is at the heart of how creation and justice relate to each other (Hanson and Williams, 2018).

But to call for and expect radical change goes against human nature, does it not, and therefore is hopelessly utopian? Yet, the Archbishop of Canterbury, Justin Welby, calls for exactly this radical change of making money serve grace in *Dethroning Mammon*, his 2017 Lenten book. God's (ridiculous) divine economics overwhelm the economics that Mammon offers us. Mammon's false implication is that money and power is all there is to be seen in this world. The answer to dethroning Mammon comes through how we measure, how we see and how we hear. Everything is to be assessed through the eyes of Jesus. Mammon tells us that there is never enough to go around, and what we have we must hold. God is all about grace and abundance. There have been times when the Kingdom of God has grown, thrived and been fruitful beyond measure. But in our own day of widespread, secular thinking, the pursuit of pleasure and the drive for material gain have all but choked it. What we receive we treat as ours. The economic wealth of historically powerful Christian countries means that the international financial system is based around the receipt of interest. How different could our world look if we thought of giving as an obligation, like our taxes, rather than a luxury extra? One of the deceits of Mammon is to pretend to lead everlasting life and eternal greatness. However, the preacher in Ecclesiastes speaks of the inability of any human being to ensure that the wealth that they have tried so hard to pile up will last (Welby, 2017). Such wealth accumulation will not lead to God's Kingdom coming. The Kingdom comes here on Earth when God, the Father, and his Son, the Lord Jesus, are honoured. The Kingdom of heaven is found among disciples as they meet together locally. The Kingdom of Heaven is among His people right across the world from every nation, language and tribe; and supremely, Christians believe, the Kingdom will come fully when the Lord Jesus returns. (Welby, 2017).

A challenge placed before Jesus, in Matthew 22:34–46, was identifying the greatest commandment. As always, Jesus moved the discussion to a new level. His answer identified God, neighbour and self, whose relationships are interconnected by love (Holder, 2017). It is in the light of this that we should view our living. We should be loving God, His Kingdom (His Creation), and loving our neighbours – always caring for their welfare in the way we live our lives.

Our Father which art in Heaven, hallowed be Thy Name; Thy Kingdom come... For all, indeed.

BIBLIOGRAPHY

Alldred N, **Some Contradictions in Community Development**, (Community Development Journal, Vol 11 No 2, 1976)

Atkinson A B, **Inequality : what can be done?** (Harvard University Press, 2015)

Bartlett J, **The People vs Tech** (Penguin Random House, 2018)

Beaumont P, Rahman A, **Scientist suggests a giant sunshade in the sky could solve global warming**, (www.theguardian.com, 2018)

Berners-Lee M, **There Is No Planet B** (Cambridge University Press, 2019)

Berry W, **The World-Ending Fire** (Penguin Random House, 2017)

Best E et al, '**Low hanging fruit: Fossil fuel Subsidies, Climate Finance, and Sustainable Development**', (Oil Change International for the Heinrich Böll Stiftung, North America, June 2012, p16)

Beynon G, **Money Counts** (The Good Book Limited, 2011)

Blomberg C L, **Neither Poverty nor Riches: A Biblical Theology of Possessions**, New Studies in Biblical Theology (Grand Rapids, MI: Eerdmans, 1999)

Bornstein D and Davis, S, **Social Entrepreneurship: What everybody needs to know** (Oxford: Oxford University Press, 2010)

Bodansky D, **The Environmental Paradox of Nuclear Power,** *Environmental Practice.* **3** (2): 86–8. doi:10.1017/S1466046600002234. (Archived from the original on 2008-01-27 [reprinted by the American Physical Society], 2001)

Bowman A, et al, **The End of the Experiment?** (Manchester Capitalism, Manchester University Press, 2014)

Bregman R, **Utopia for Realists** (Bloomsbury Publishing PLC, 2017)

Brennan J, **Against Democracy** (Princeton Press, 2016)

Brooks R, **The Great Tax Robbery** (Oneworld Publications, 2013)

Chancel, L. and Piketty, T., **Carbon and inequality: From Kyoto to Paris**, (Paris School of Economics, 2015).

Carey J, **Melbourne Desalination Plant**, (www.dailymail.co.uk , 2018)

Chilton D, **Productive Christians in an Age of Guilt Manipulators** (Institute of Christian Economics, 1982)

Cocker M, **Rivers of Blood; Rivers of Gold: Europe's conflict with Tribal Peoples** (Pimlico, 1999)

Conway G, **One Billion Hungry: Can we feed the world**? (Cornell: Cornell University Press, 2012)

Coote, A and Goodwin, N, **The Great Transition: Social Justice and the Core Economy**, (NEF working paper 1, London: New Economics Foundation, 2010)

Corporate European Observatory, **Life Beyong Emissions Trading**, (2014)

Cronon W, **Wilderness preserves and decimation of indigenous peoples**: (1995)

Current Population Annual Social and Economic Supplement: Historic Income Tables (Table F-5) and Bureau of Labour Statistics, Productivity – Major Sector Productivity and Costs Database, (2012.

Dreze J and Sen A, **Hunger and Public Action** (New York: Oxford University Press, 1989)

Duncan G J, **Economic Costs of Early Childhood Poverty** (2008)

Eagleton T F, **Marx was Right** (Yale University Press, 2011)

Easterly W, **The White Man's Burden** (New York: Penguin Books, 2006)

Englebert C, **Robots** (Post in LinkedIn, 2017)

Faller P, **The way children travel** (Fresh from the Word, 2018)

Fullerton J, **The Big Choice**, (Capital Institute, July 19, 2011)

Give Directly, **2012 Annual Report** (https://www.givedirectly.org/pdf/2012AnnualReport.pdf,7.)

https://dash.harvard.edu/bitstream/handle/1/4412631/ClemensPlace Premium.pdf?sequence=1)

https://www.theguardian.com/news/datablog/2012/may/24/robert-kennedy-gdp.

https://neweconomics.org/2009/05/guide-social-return-investment

Grayling A C, **Democracy and its Crisis** (Oneworld Publications, 2017)

Gregg R, **Important Last Words** (Sermon in 2017)

Hamilton N, **Global Morality** (Presbyterian Herald, 2017)

Hanlon J, et al, **Just Give Money to the Poor** (Kumarian Press, University of Manchester , 2010)

Hanson J and Williams M, **True Marks of Mission** (Presbyterian Herald, 2018)

Harari Y, **Homo Deus** , (Harvill Secker, 2015)

Hardin G, **The Tragedy of the Commons**, (Science, 1968)

Hickel J, **The Divide**, (Penguin Random House Group, 2017)

Higgs D, **Honesty and the NHS** (Letter to The Guardian, 2018)

Holder J, **Jesus – challenged and challenging** (Fresh from the Word, IBRA, 2017)

Hough J and Rice B, **Providing Personalised Support to Rough Sleepers. An Evaluation of the City of London Project** (Joseph Rowntree Foundation , 2010)

Huddleston T Jnr, '**Sean Parker wonders what Facebook is "Doing to Our Children's Brains**"', www.fortune.com, 9/11/17 (Bartlett, 2018, p18).

Hughes C, **Fair Shot: rethinking inequality and how we earn** (Bloomsbury Publishing PLC, 2018)

Jackson T, **Prosperity without Growth** (Sustainable Development Commission, 2017)

Joseph Rowntree Foundation, **Providing personalised support to rough sleepers**: An evaluation of the City of London pilot (2010)

Klein N, **This Changes Everything** (Allen Lane, 2014)

Kendall J and Voorhies R, **The Mobile Finance Revolution**, (Foreign Affairs, March/April 2014, 9 and 10)

Kibasi T, et al, **Prosperity and Justice: A plan for the new economy** (IPPR Commission On Economic Justice Report 2018)

King M, **The End of Alchemy** (Little Brown Book Group Limited, 2016)

Kingsnorth P, **Confessions of a Recovering Environmentalist** (Faber & Faber, 2017)

Levitt S and Dubner S, **Super Freakonomics** (Allen Lane, 2009)

Liogier R, **France's Neither Nor Election** (The New York Times, 2017)

Mandeville B, **The Fable of the Bees** (1714)

Marmot M, **The Health Gap : The Challenge of an Unequal World** (Bloomsbury, 2015)

Mencken H L, **Notes on Democracy**, (Knopf, 1926)

Milanovic B, **Global Inequality : A New Approach for the Age of Globalisation** (Harvard University Press, 2016)

Minsky H, **The Financial Instability Hypothesis** (Challenge, March-April 1977)

Moore J, The Independent, March 24, 2015).

Monbiot G, **The Age of Consent** (Flamingo, 2003)

Montesquieu, Charles-Louis de Secondat, Baron de, **The Spirit of Laws** (1748)

Mueller J, **Capitalism, Peace and the Historical Movement of Ideas** (International Interactions, 2010)

McLeish T, **Faith & Wisdom in Science** (Oxford University Press, 2014)

Naish J, **Enough: Breaking Free from the World of Excess**, (Hodder and Stoughton, 2009)

New Economic Foundation, <https://neweconomics.org/2009/05/guide-

social-return-investment>

Nicholson P, **Look around, not up** (Fresh from the Word, IBRA, 2018)

Nussbaum M, **Capabilities approach**, Harvard University Press, 2000).

Ormerod P, **Butterfly Economics** (Faber & Faber, 1999)

Picket K, **Inequality** (British Medical Journal, BMJ 2017;356:j556)

Piketty T, **Capital in the Twenty-First Century** (Harvard University Press, 2014)

Pinker S, **Enlightenment Now: The Case for Reason, Science, Humanism and Progress** (Allen Lane, 2018)

Preston G, **Christian Joy** (Sermon in 2009)

Profit Shifting and 'Aggressive' Tax Planning by Multinational Firms,(Centre for European Economic Research, October 2013, p3).

Raworth K, **Doughnut Economics** (Penguin Random House, 2017)

Rosenfeld S, **Democracy and Truth: A Short History** (Pensylvania, 2018)

Rookes P, **Commitment, Conscience or Compromise: the financial basis and evolving role of Christian Health Services in developing countries** (Lambert Academic Publishing, 2012)

Rousseau J J, **Discourse on Inequality** (1754)

Sachs J, **The End of Poverty** (Penguin Books Ltd, 2005)

Sacks J, **Morality in the 21st century** (The Daily Telegraph and BBC Radio 4, 2018)

Said E, **Orientalism**, (Pantheon Books, 1978)

Sanderson R, **Social Injustice** (Presbyterian Herald, 2017)

Sider R, **Rich Christians in an Age of Hunger** (W Publishing Group, Sixth Edition, 2015)

Spencer N, **The Political Samaritan: how power hijacked a parable** (Bloomsbury, 2018)

Stern N, **The Economics of Climate Change**: The Stern Review (Cambridge, Cambridge University Press, (2006), xviii.)

Stiglitz J, **Globalization and Its Discontents** (Penguin Books, 2002)

Stiglitz J, **Making Globilization Work** (Allen Lane, 2006)

Suzman J, **Affluence without Abundance** (Bloomsbury, 2017)

The World Ultra Wealth Report 2017, Exclusive UHNWI Analysis (5th Ed) June 27,2017)

The proliferation of high-net-worth individuals, (The Economist: Oct 4, 2017).

Transparency International, **Corruption Perception Index 2016** (2016)

Tocqueville de A, **Democracy in America** (1835)

Todaro M, **Economic Development** (1994), 590.

Venetoullis J and Cubb C, **The Genuine Progress Indicator 1950-2002** (Oakland: Redefining Progress, 2004)

Wallace, S., **Rain Forest for Sale**, (National Geographic, Jan 2013)

Walmsley T et al; **Measuring the impact of the movement of labour using a model of bilateral migration flows**; (World Bank, 2006)

Weiss, D. J., **Big Oil's Lust for Tax Loopholes**, (Centre for American Progress, Jan 31, 2011)

Welby J, **Dethroning Mammon: Making Money Serve Grace** (Bloomsbury, 2017)

Wilkinson R and Picket K, **The Spirit Level** (London: Penguin Books Ltd, 2011)

Williams M, **Blessed are the Poor?** (Presbyterian Herald, 2016)

World Economic and Social Survey 2011: '**The Great Green Technological Transformation**', (UN Dept of ESA, 2011, ppxxii, 174).

Worstall T, **Why Thomas Piketty's Global Wealth Tax Won't Work**, (Forbes, March 30, 2014).

Wright R, **A Short History of Progress** (House of Anansi Press, 2004)

www.geoengineering.ox.ac.uk, (2018)

www.gallop.com/poll/124028/700-million-worldwide-desiremigrate-permantly.aspx.

Varoufakis Y, **And The Weak Suffer What They Must?** (Penguin Random House, 2016)

Zucman G, **The Missing Wealth of Nations**, Quarterly Journal of Economics 128, no 3(2013): 1321-64

Zucman G; Torslov T; Weir L, **The Policy Failure of High-Tax Countries** (National Bureau of Economic Research, Working Papers. pp. 44–49, June 2018)

ACKNOWLEDGEMENTS

MY GREAT THANKS TO good friends Nicky McBride, Dr Howard Welch and Leslie Carswell for agreeing to read the early drafts. Thanks to other friends, who entered into friendly and helpful discussion that was wide-ranging, namely – Eugene Neeson, Michael Glass, Alasdair Kyle, Nigel McBride, Graeme Allen, John Barnett and David Adams. Very useful reading suggestions and guidance came from Emma Bonnar, Richard Bonnar and Moira Kyle. Also I want to thank Dr Peter Rookes, David Scott, Dr Jonny Hanson, and Rev Dr Alan Russell for insightful assistance ranging from ecology to theology. With the study of mathematics and French in my distant past, I am indebted in this area to Hilary Taylor, Philip McGivern, John Hope, and Ruth Graham.

Special thanks to Neil Alldred for detailed analysis of the text, stimulating discussions and his guidance through the additional relevant background reading, which I had initially overlooked. My thanks also go to Clare Hutchinson for editing assistance and to Dr Wesley Johnston and all the staff at Colourpoint Creative Ltd. And finally thanks of course to my wife, Joanne, and my family for their forbearance over 4 years.

APPENDIX 1

Recommendations:

Personal				
Kate Raworth	**Ron Sider**	**Mervyn King**	**Steven Pinker**	**Wendell Berry**
Rooftops that grow food	Walk, bike, carpool, use public transport	Raise national saving and investment		Learn the sources and costs of our economic lives
Renewable energy microgrids	Reduce, reuse, recycle			Understand radical limits
Open source circular economy network of innovators	Fuel efficient vehicles			Cultivate a sympathetic as well as a rational mind
	Use airplanes less			
	"Theology of enough"			
	Ethical investing			

Personal				
Graham Beynon	**Paul Kingsnorth**	**Richard Brooks**	**Rutger Bergman**	**A C Grayling**
Pay off private debt	Withdrawing			
Balance your budget	Preserve non-human life by re-wilding			
Give generously - locally and globally	Get your hands dirty			
Beware greed	Build refuges			

175

TOWARDS OIKOS

Personal				
Chris Hughes	**Jamie Bartlett**	**Thomas Piketty**	**Naomi Klein**	**Tony Atkinson**
	Own your opinion		speak out prophetically to educate about the externalisation of costs	
	Fight technological distraction		local plant based diet	
	Develop a new digital ethics		fly less	
	Smash your echo chamber		smaller environmental footprints	

Personal				
Joseph Stiglitz	**George Monbiot**	**Manchester capitaliam**	**Mark Dick**	
			Civic education to combat "flimsy news"	
			Break out of personal "bubbles" and take a global view	

National				
Kate Raworth	**Ron Sider**	**Mervyn King**	**Steven Pinker**	**Wendell Berry**
Higher-tax, higher-return public sector	Cut all greenhouse gas emissions	Safe and liquid 'narrow' banks	Nuclear fusion to power desalination plants (in the future?)	Clean up our own messes
Progressive water rates	Renewable energy research	Risky illiquid 'wide' banks	Capturing and storing carbon dioxide	Make locally adapted economies
Land value taxes	Stop Damage to marginal lands	Central Bank as a Pawnbroker For All Seasons		
Green QE	Government organised Land reform	Tax on the degree of alchemy		
Basic personal income	Boost Overseas Development Aid above 0.7% of Gross national Income	Move away from an economy of domestic spending towards exports		
Encourage complementary currencies to boost local economies and reward unpaid work				

APPENDIX 1 - RECOMMENDATIONS

Rooted membership and shakeholder finance for employees				
Tax the use of non-renewable resources instead of labour				
Royalities from co-owned public-private patents				
Invest in teaching social entrepreneurship/ problem solving				
Public knowledge of all public funded research				

National				
Graham Beynon	**Paul Kingsnorth**	**Richard Brooks**	**Rutger Bergman**	**A C Grayling**
		jettison HMRC - big business cosy relationship	Basic income	transparency about individuals in elections
		tear up UK/ Switzerland tax agreement	Fifteen-Hour Workweek	transparency about funding in elections
				fact-check monitoring
				ban betting on elections
				compulsory voting with civic education
				proportional representation
			Open Borders	political party whipping only on manifesto commitments

177

National				
Chris Hughes	**Jamie Bartlett**	**Thomas Piketty**	**Naomi Klein**	**Tony Atkinson**
targeted basic income	Teach critical thinking		use power as voter, consumer, investor to prioritise relationship	technological innovation to increase the employability of workers
	Police the algorithms			A Social and Economic Council
	Break the Ad model			Guaranteed public employment at the minimum wage
	Update election campaign laws			national pay policy with statutatory living wage
	Hold a pre-election celebration day			national savings bonds at guaranteed real rate of interest on savings (Maximum holding)
	Bot-watch			capital endownment to all at adulthood
				public investment authority operating a sovereign wealth fund
				progressive structure for personal income tax, up to top rate at 65%, with broad tax base
				Earned Income Discount to first band of earnings
				inheritance and gifts taxed under a progressive lifetime capital receipts tax
				progressive property tax
				credit market for borrowing not secured on housing
				income-based-tax treatment of private pension contributions

APPENDIX 1 – RECOMMENDATIONS

National				
Joseph Stiglitz	**Goerge Monbiot**	**Manchester capitalism**	**Mark Dick**	
		decentralise the state	Replace NHS "free at point of care" with 2% real cost charge	
		conduct economic experiments in the foundational economy	Tax the retired with annual income above £65000 at 40% and 65% rate	
		social licensing withing a learning state	Retrospective university education tax	
			Government cash grabs into excessive occupational pensions	
			Sensible mansion and rental income property taxes	
			Pay off public (national) debt first	
			Open borders	

International				
Kate Raworth	**Ron Sider**	**Mervyn King**	**Steven Pinker**	**Wendell Berry**
End tax loopholes, offshore havens	Carbon taxes phased in	Reinvigorate the IMF		Stop breaking ecological things we cannot fix
Tax accumulated wealth	International pollution standards upheld	Permanent swap aggreements among central banks		Abandon the delusion the more industrialisation will repair industrialisation/ globalisation
shorten paid working week	Microfinance	Accept floating exchange rates		Quit 'moving on' - geographically, historically and ecologically
New ranking metrics for G20 instead of GDP	Support for public health and education in developing countries	Return to normal real interest rates		
High taxation for the use of environmental resources such as water and oil	Adopt the Genuine Progress Indicator as a new metric	Restructure sovereign debts		
tax on pollutants	All large corporations to endorse International Labour Organisation conventions	Boost resource productivity		

Heavily tax aviation travel	Emphasise developing country ownership of ODA decisions	Promotion of free trade		
Creation of Commons Trusts on a global scale				
Global tax on extreme personal wealth				
Global financial transaction tax to reign in high-frequency trading				
"Patient capital" for renewable energy technologies and public transport systems				
Living metrics for businesses via the MultiCapital Scorecard				

International				
Graham Beynon	Paul Kingsnorth	Richard Brooks	Rutger Bergman	A C Grayling
		disclosure of tax payments via world wide financial reporting standard		
		global tax on capital wealth, investments, shares and dividends		

International				
Chris Hughes	Jamie Bartlett	Thomas Piketty	Naomi Klein	Tony Atkinson
	Spread the wealth	Global financial transparancy	agroecology	universal Child Benefit
	Robot taxes		full commitment to renewable energies	Participation Income (a basic guaranteed income for all)
	New safty nets (?UBI)			Rich countries to increase Overseas Development Aid to 1% of Gross National Income
	Worker's rights	progressive global tax on capital		global wealth tax

APPENDIX 1 – RECOMMENDATIONS

	Fair trade browsing			
	Anti--trust			
	Safe Artifical Intelligence			
	The transparent leviathan			
	Regulate Bitcoin		Polluter pays	
	Plan future government			

International				
Joseph Stiglitz	**George Monbiot**	**Manchester capitalism**	**Mark Dick**	
fairer trade regime	A Fair Trade Organisation		UN facilitating new international deliberative democracy for debate and discussion	
new approach to intellectual property promoting research	An International Clearing Union		Dissolve the EU and other trading blocks and adopt real free trade	
compensating countries for their environmental services	A World Parliament		UN General Assembly directly elected by populations rather than nomonated by governments	
lower carbon emissions everywhere			UN General Assembly seats available to regions via proportional representation	
fair payment to developing countries for their natural resources			UN General Assembly to control global UBI fund of $30 trillion	
0.7% GDP ODA from all developed nations				
international debt forgiveness				
a global reserve system				
multinational corporations to confront their liabilities from damage to the environment				
support democracy				

APPENDIX 2

IN 1906 THE ITALIAN engineer and economist Vilfredo Pareto proposed, via statistical analysis, that eighty per cent of a country's wealth is held by about twenty per cent of the people. This departure from an egalitarian state, where each fraction of a population x owns the same fraction of wealth y, was expressed by him in the mathematical formula:

$ln(y) = ln(A) + n\,ln(x)$

Here A is a constant. If one takes the exponent of this expression and demands that $y = 0$ at $x = 0$ and $y = 1$ at $x = 1$, there results the power law:

$y = x^n$

One knows from calculus that its derivative is $dy/dx = nx^{n-1}$ and, hence, y satisfies the first order differential expression:

$dy/dx = n \div x \times y$ subject to $y(1) = 1$

If we plot this function for values of n = 1, 2, 4, 8, and 16, we get the wealth distribution curves shown:

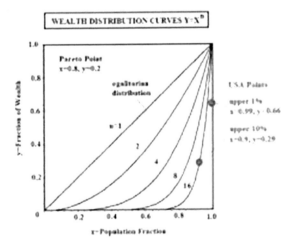

182

In an ideal egalitarian state the curve corresponding to n = 1 holds while in a totalitarian state, where all power lies with just one person, the n = ∞ case applies. The curves in between refer to populations with different degrees of wealth distribution.

This distribution is seen to be highly slanted towards the very wealthy and is in excess of the 20–80 rule described by Pareto, which corresponds to n = 8. The upper 1% of the US population is seen to control about 34% of the wealth and the upper 10% controls a total of 71% of the wealth, as indicated by the red dots in the graph. This distribution is thus seen to be close to the Pareto curve $y = x^{16}$ with the very richest 1% requiring an even larger exponent of $n = 32$.

APPENDIX 3

BASE EROSION AND PROFIT shifting (BEPS) refers to tax avoidance strategies that exploit gaps and mismatches in tax rules to artificially shift profits to low or no-tax locations. Under the OECD/G20 Inclusive Framework on BEPS, over 125 countries and jurisdictions are collaborating to implement the BEPS measures and tackle BEPS. The aim of the project is to mitigate tax code loopholes and country-to-country inconsistencies so that corporations cannot shift profits from a country with a high corporate tax rate to countries with a low tax rate. The practice - in particular double non-taxation - is usually legal but often involves complex manoeuvres within tax law. BEPS is costly for all parties involved, save the firm. The citizens' trust in tax systems can be harmed by widespread tax avoidance practices, which puts at stake fiscal consent a concept at the core of modern democracies; it is also a loss of revenues for the State. A conservative estimate has annual tax revenue losses between 100 and US$240 billion (i.e. 4–10% of global revenues from corporate income tax) due to profit shifting around the globe.

Some corporations while using OECD-whitelisted tools, IP-based BEPS (base erosion and profit shifting) tools and Debt-based BEPS tools, don't file public accounts. This enables the corporates to avoid taxes, not just in the corporate haven, but in all operating countries that have tax treaties with the haven (Centre for European Economic Research, 2013). Smaller corporate havens meet the IMF definition of offshore financial centres, as the untaxed accounting flows from the BEPS tools artificially distort the economic statistics of the haven (e.g. Ireland›s 2015 leprechaun economics GDP and Luxembourg›s seventy per cent GNI to GDP ratio are in the top fifteen per cent of the GDP-per-capita tax haven proxy list).

GLOSSARY

AI – In computer science, **artificial intelligence** (**AI**), sometimes called **machine** intelligence, is intelligence demonstrated by machines, in contrast to the natural intelligence displayed by humans and animals.

AIDS – acquired immune deficiency syndrome is the name used to describe a number of potentially life-threatening infections and illnesses that happen when your immune system has been severely damaged by the HIV virus.

Christians Against Poverty (CAP) is a Christian charitable company in the United Kingdom founded in Bradford, West Yorkshire by John Kirkby in 1996.

DEMOS is Britain's leading cross-party think-tank. We produce original research, publish innovative thinkers and host thought-provoking events.

EU Savings Tax Directive is a directive of the European Union enacted to implement the European Union withholding tax, requiring member states to provide other member states with information on interest paid to achieve effective taxation of the payments in the member state where the taxpayer is resident for tax purposes.

Eurogroup is the recognised collective term for informal meetings of the finance ministers of the eurozone – those member states of the European Union (EU) which have adopted the euro as their official currency.

FATCA – The **Foreign Account Tax Compliance Act** (**FATCA**) is a 2010 United States federal law requiring all non-U.S. foreign financial institutions (FFIs) to search their records for customers with indicia of U.S.-person status, being indications in records of a U.S. place of birth, prior residency, or similar.

Feed the Future – The Feed the Future Initiative was launched in 2010 by the United States government and the Obama Administration to address global hunger and food insecurity.

GiveDirectly is a non-profit organization operating in East Africa that helps families living in extreme poverty by making unconditional cash transfers to them via mobile phone.

GDP – Gross Domestic Product is a monetary measure of the market value of all the final goods and services produced in a period of time, often annually.

GPI – A **genuine progress indicator** is a metric used to measure the economic growth of a country. It is often considered an alternative metric to the more well known gross domestic product (GDP) economic **indicator**.

GFI – Global Financial Integrity works to curtail illicit financial flows by producing groundbreaking research, promoting pragmatic policy solutions, and advising governments.

G7 – The Group of Seven (G7) is a group consisting of Canada, France, Germany, Italy, Japan, the United Kingdom, and the United States. These countries, with the seven largest IMF-described advanced economies in the world, represent 58% of the global net wealth ($317 trillion).

HBSC – one of the largest banking and financial services institutions in the world, serves millions of customers through its four Global Businesses.

International Clearing Union was one of the institutions proposed to be set up at the 1944 United Nations Monetary and Financial Conference at Bretton Woods, New Hampshire, in the United States, by British economist John Maynard Keynes.

IMF – The International Monetary Fund (IMF) is an international organization headquartered in Washington, D.C., consisting of 189 countries working to foster global monetary cooperation, secure financial stability, facilitate international trade, promote high employment and sustainable economic growth, and reduce poverty around the world.

IPPR – The Institute for Public Policy Research is a left-wing think tank based in London.

LODR – lender of last resort is the institution in a financial system that acts as the provider of liquidity to a financial institution which finds itself unable to obtain sufficient liquidity in the interbank lending market and other facilities or sources have been exhausted.

MDGs – The United Nations Millennium Declaration, signed in September 2000 commits world leaders to combat poverty, hunger, disease, illiteracy, environmental degradation, and discrimination against women.

M-Peso is a mobile phone-based money transfer, financing and microfinancing service, launched in 2007 by Vodafone for Safaricom and Vodacom, the largest mobile network operators in Kenya and Tanzania.

MIT – The Massachusetts Institute of Technology is a private research university in Cambridge, Massachusetts.

MultiCapital Scorecard is a free and open-source management tool (a public good) that organizations can use to measure, manage and report their performance in a fully integrated (Triple Bottom Line) way.

NEF – **The New Economics Foundation** (**NEF**) is a British think-tank that promotes "social, economic and environmental justice". **NEF** was founded in 1986 by the leaders of The Other Economic Summit (TOES) with the aim of working for a «new model of wealth creation, based on equality, diversity and economic stability».

NIMBY – an acronym for the phrase "Not In My Back Yard" is a characterization of opposition by residents to a proposed development in their local area.

OECD – The Organisation for Economic Co-operation and Development is an intergovernmental economic organisation with 36 member countries, founded in 1961.

ODA – **Official development aid** is a term coined by the Development Assistance Committee (DAC) of the Organisation for Economic Co-operation and Development (OECD) to measure aid.

OPEC is defined as an abbreviation for Organization of Petroleum Exporting Countries, which is a union of oil producing countries that regulate the amount of oil each country is able to produce.

Open Source Circular Economy is an embodiment of two concepts; open source applied to circular economy. It reposes on transparency, reuse, reducing waste, generating economic development and transforming what is waste from one product into the input for other products and services in a very scarce, vulnerable and degradable environment.

Populism – movement claiming to support the interests of the ordinary people. Sometimes defined as the equitable redistribution of wealth and power, which advances policies that reflect the values, beliefs, needs, interests and wishes of the common people.

QE – Quantitative Easing is a monetary policy whereby a central bank buys predetermined amounts of government bonds or other financial assets in order to inject money directly into the economy.

RCT – **randomised control trial** is a **trial** in which subjects are randomly assigned to one of two groups: one (the experimental group) receiving the intervention that is being tested, and the other (the comparison group or **control**) receiving an alternative (conventional) treatment.

SAP – Structural adjustment programs (SAPs) consist of loans provided by the International Monetary Fund (IMF) and the World Bank (WB) to countries that experienced economic crises which then forces them to concentrate more on trade and production so it can boost their economy.

SROI – Social return on investment is a principles-based method for measuring extra-financial value (such as environmental or social value) not currently reflected or involved in conventional financial accounts.

Transparency International is the global civil society organisation leading the fight against corruption.

Tyndall Centre – The Tyndall Centre for Climate Change Research is an organisation based in the United Kingdom that brings together scientists, economists, engineers and social scientists.

UBI – Universal Basic Income is a periodic cash payment delivered to all on an individual basis, without means test or work requirement.

Universal Credit is replacing 6 other benefits with a single monthly payment if you 're out of work or on a low income.

UN WTO – The World Tourism Organization is the United Nations specialized agency responsible for the promotion of responsible, sustainable and universally accessible tourism.

Washington Consensus is a set of 10 economic policy prescriptions considered to constitute the "standard" reform package promoted for crisis-wracked developing countries by Washington, D.C.-based institutions such as the International Monetary Fund (IMF), World Bank and United States Department of the Treasury.

World Bank – (French: Banque mondiale) is an international financial institution that provides loans to countries of the world for capital projects.

WNA – The World Nuclear Association is the international organization that promotes nuclear power and supports the companies that comprise the global nuclear industry.

WTO – The World Trade Organization is an intergovernmental organization that is concerned with the regulation of international trade between nations.

World Vision UK is an international charity devoted to improving the lives of the most vulnerable children.

Zero Hunger Programme pledges to end hunger, achieve food security, improve nutrition and promote sustainable agriculture, and is the priority of the World Food Programme.

QUESTIONNAIRE

On a scale of 0-10 where 0 is "Nil" or "Not at all" and 10 is "Completely", how has your perception of the following issues changed after reading 'Towards Oikos'

1   Your **knowledge** of inequality issues?

    BEFORE .....   AFTER .....

2   Your **knowledge** of climate crisis issues?

    BEFORE .....   AFTER .....

3   How concerned are you about equality of opportunity for all?

    BEFORE.....   AFTER .....

4   How persuaded are you for the need to deal with global warming?

    BEFORE .....   AFTER .....

5   How likely are you to **decide** to make lifestyle changes addressing inequality?

    BEFORE .....   AFTER .....